W9-AZJ-618

THE LAZY GARDENER'S GARDEN BOOK

THE LAZY GARDENER'S
GARDEN BOOK

WILLIAM MORWOOD

Illustrations by Sharon Landa

Gramercy Publishing Company · New York

51711464X
Copyright © MCMLXX by William Morwood
Library Of Congress Catalog Card Number: 69-15175
All rights reserved.
This edition is published by Gramercy Books
a division of Crown Publishers, Inc.
by arrangement with Doubleday and Company, Inc.
a b c d e f g h
Manufactured in the United States Of America

CONTENTS

Section Three — Shrub Maintenance

Section Four — Flower Maintenance

Section Five — Ground Cover Maintenance

INTRODUCTION

Most garden books are written for people who love to garden, who have green thumbs and an unrestrained passion for little growing things.

This book is not for them.

This book is for people who have brown thumbs, plenty of restraint about little growing things, and a passion for getting through garden chores fast so they can move on to something more interesting.

Don't get us wrong. Lazy Gardeners aren't all bad. They're self-respecting members of the community and they don't really mean it when they threaten to pour green concrete to replace patchy front lawns. Like everybody else they love beautiful things, including gardens, and they secretly envy the lady up the street. What a place she has—well-pruned trees, manicured shrubs, gorgeous flowers. But my God, the time she puts in! Seems like she does nothing else but.

The Lazy Gardener, leafing through the home magazines, sees illustrations of show gardens and gets depressed. He doesn't need to be told that behind that society woman, pictured on a velvet lawn backed by a rainbow of flowers, stands an army of unseen yard men. The special articles don't cheer him up either. Those luscious photographs of roses, with dew still fresh on them, make ordinary gardeners drool. But the Lazy Gardener remains dry-mouthed and tight-lipped. He knows all about roses. He tried them once—to the delight of every biting, chewing, and sucking insect in the neighborhood.

He wonders wistfully if there's any way to achieve a modicum of what he wants in a garden without developing gnarled hands and a pretzel look from stooping.

The hopeful message of this book is that we believe there is a way. We believe that, with a little planning, a relaxed schedule of maintenance chores can be worked out which will result in a rewarding garden with minimum effort.

If the words "planning" and "schedule" frighten you, consider a minute. You're accustomed to a more or less planned schedule for your other maintenance activities. If you're the woman of the house, you launder, vacuum, and dust on certain days of the week or month. If you're the man, you gas up the car, wash it, and have it lubricated according to certain signs and signals which urge you into action. Neither of you need be too rigid about your timing. A day or two early or late doesn't make all that difference (except for gas). The point is that, in one way or another, you've worked out a comfortable pattern for chores, spacing them so that everything doesn't have to be done all at once.

Why not the same relaxed pattern for garden maintenance? Your plants will love you for it. A spaced-out schedule over an entire season meets their growing needs much better than furious activity concentrated into a few spring weekends.

Here's where my compulsive Green Thumber makes a mistake. He thinks that by working up a storm in spring he can fortify his garden against later neglect. And so he goes at it with relentless vigor—liming, cultivating, fertilizing, blistering hands, straining muscles. Sometimes he slips a disc and is totally out of action when the hot weather comes—a time when his plants need him most to help fight off the three grim reapers—fungus, pests, and drought.

As a Lazy Gardener, you don't aim to slip a disc and you're a better plant friend because of it. Your idea of what to do on a fine spring day is a drive in the country, not roughing it in the garden. That's fine with your plants; in spring they have everything going for them anyway. You're willing to perform a certain minimum of maintenance chores from time to time, but that's it. Again your plants have no objection—*if* you perform what they need when they need it. In summer heat you want to spend idle hours relaxing in a hammock. Your plants are delighted, but they argue, reasonably enough, that if you relax with a cool drink in hand, you should at least give a passing thought to *their* thirst needs.

In short, with good will and tolerance on either side, you and your plants can become natural allies in the gardening venture. It is the purpose of this book to explore some of the problems which may arise in the course of your relationship and to suggest solutions which may help to promote a better understanding between you.

THE LAZY GARDENER'S GARDEN BOOK

Lawn Maintenance

Chapter 1

LAWN GRASSES

Suppose you were a grass plant growing in your own lawn. You'd find things pretty crowded down there. Forty to sixty of you are squashed into a single foot of ground. You're in competition for light and air, food and water, and if that isn't bad enough, you get your head chopped off regularly once a week.

No wonder as the season drags along you lose strength and get pushed aside by crabgrass and other burly weeds conditioned to knuckles and knees fighting. By midsummer you're further weakened by grubs and weevils chewing at your roots and, if you still survive, you have little stamina left to fight off the fungus diseases which come drifting in on the August winds.

You're a self-respecting, proud little grass plant. You'd like to grow vigorously, to become a healthy unit in a luscious green lawn. But under the artificial circumstances of your environment, you're just not able to make it without help.

Even as a Lazy Gardener, doesn't this factual account of what's happening out in your greensward cut you to the quick, no matter how slow your quick may be? You probably want to rush out and do something about it right away. But restrain yourself. You won't be able to help your grasses until you know them better. Let's start by finding out their names.

GRASS IDENTIFICATION

If you live in the northern two-thirds of the nation, chances are good that the predominant grass in your lawn is Kentucky Bluegrass or one of its varieties—upright-growing, tufted plants.

Bluegrass

If you live in Florida, the Deep South or Southwest, your lawn could be Bermuda, St. Augustine, Zoysia, or even Dichondra (which isn't a grass at all)—all sideways-growing, recumbent plants.

Bermuda

But just to complicate matters, in each region there are areas where, for one reason or another, the prevailing grasses do poorly and other types have been introduced. So we had better make sure of the basic grass in your lawn before we go further. As you will see later, a lot depends on it.

Two methods are open for your grass identification:

Method #1 Ask a Green Thumb Neighbor

This is a good bet if his lawn looks like you want yours to look some day. But be wary. Green Thumbers often talk in a high-flown botanical language which can confuse more than enlighten you.

Method #2 Take a Turf Sample to Your Garden Center

This is the more reliable and recommended method. When we speak of "your" Garden Center we're assuming that you've scouted your neighborhood and found the emporium best suited to your needs and temperament. If its owner or one of his salesmen is knowledgeable and sympathetic, you're in special luck. Many garden problems are outside the scope of this book and it's invaluable to have an authority close at hand to consult about them.

Be sure to dig out a large enough turf sample to make identification possible—at least a foot square and two inches thick. Carve it from the healthiest section of your lawn, since a sample that's half weeds can be misleading. After your Garden Center salesman has identified the desirable grasses, you can take the turf home and slip it back into its old slot in your lawn where it'll be none the worse for its outing.

Don't be concerned if every last blade of grass isn't identified. The basic type is the important one. Others in a lawn mix were chosen because they co-exist with it. What's good for Basic is good for them.

Turf sample

Chapter 2

___

MOWING

Now that you've identified your basic turfgrass and can call it by name—"Hi there, Bluegrass!"—you're ready to cut your lawn. We know it's full of weeds and bare patches, but you're going to cut it anyway. Nothing is more important for the future health and looks of your lawn than developing a correct mowing technique.

Lawn grasses flourish best when cut at a height best suited to their growth habits. The upward-growing (tufted) grasses— Bluegrasses, Ryes, Fescues—must be cut comparatively high since they need top growth to manufacture food. To cut them lower than recommended is to invite weakening of the plants and the eventual wiping out of your lawn by diseases they will be unable to resist.

Sideways-growing (recumbent) grasses have a different problem. Their leaves and stems move along close to the ground, too low to be reached by mowing blades. At least for a while. But rapidly, during a single growing season, this growth piles up, layer on layer, until all light is cut off from the lower tiers. So recumbent grasses—Bermudas, St. Augustine, Bents—must be cut *low* to keep them cleaned out. To cut higher than recommended is to encourage a buildup of "thatch" which eventually becomes so impenetrable that water and fertilizers won't reach the roots. In course of time the grass will dry out, brown out and die.

Look at the following table, pick your grass and note the recommended cutting height.

Type of Grass	Cutting Height
Bluegrasses	
(Or mixtures where Bluegrass predominates)	1½ inches
Ryegrasses	
(Or mixtures where Ryegrass predominates)	1½ inches
Fescues	
(Or mixtures where Fescues predominate)	1½ inches
Bent Grasses	
(Or mixtures where Bents predominate)	½ inch
Bermudas	
(Common or hybrid)	½ inch
Zoysia Grasses	¾ inch
St. Augustine Grass	
(Also Kikuyu Grass—the Lord pity you)	¾ inch

LAWN MOWERS

Unless you have a goat with height adjustable teeth, you're going to cut your grass with a lawn mower. The only question is, which type—reel or rotary?

Reel type mower

The reel type works with a downward spinning action, catching the grass between its blades and the bottom plate of the machine, shearing it off in a continuous sequence of strokes. Rotaries work on another principle. A single blade whirls around at great speed, beheading all grass within reach.

Rotary mower

Which is preferable?

Whichever you have now is just dandy. But if you're un-committed, or the time ever comes when you must buy a new one, opt for the reel type. Reasons: smoother cut, better control of cutting height, less damage to grass because of crisper surgery.

ADJUSTING THE CUTTING HEIGHT

If you're really a Lazy Gardener and not just faking, you'll load your machine into the trunk of your car and drive to the nearest lawn-mower repair shop. Along with getting a height adjustment, you might also get the blades sharpened and the machine oiled and cleaned.

If you're a home mechanic (and you *still* could be a Lazy Gardener at that) place the mower on a hard surface, like the garage floor, while you're making the adjustments. Use a stiff-edged ruler to measure up the desired height from the floor.

HOW TO MOW A LAWN

Yes, Virginia, there is a trick to mowing a lawn. Those smooth, stripe-cut greens you see on golf courses don't just happen by accident. Smart professional brains have been at work, devising the most efficient way of getting the grass out of there, and we could do a lot worse than steal from them.

The problem works down to this—how to imagine your lawn as a rectangle, if it isn't one already. If it's a geometrically com-plex lawn, with a lot of twists and turns, try to imagine it as a series of contiguous rectangles, joined together on at least one side.

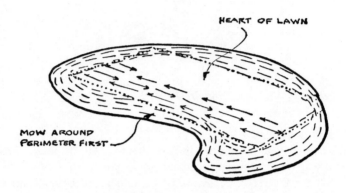

HEART OF LAWN

MOW AROUND
PERIMETER FIRST

These rectangles are the "heart" of your lawn. By mowing up and down them, with about a one-third overlap, you're going to get that smooth "professional" look—if not at the first cutting, then later in the season.

But what are you going to do about all those leftovers outside the rectangles?

You're going to dispose of them *first*—mowing around the outer perimeter until all the "leftovers" have been cleared off. Only then will you be ready for the straight cuts, the up and down sweeps (overlapping one-third) which will leave your lawn patterned (if you use a reel mower) in attractive ribbons of green and gray—green where the machine pushed the grass toward you, gray where it pushed away, exposing the under sides of the leaves.

Don't be too indignant if you find that, because of the original perimeter mowing, you are cutting patches of grass twice over. Some enthusiasts have been known to cut an entire lawn twice over—deliberately—criss-crossing the second cut over the first—though, needless to say, such people have long since been black-balled from the Lazy Gardeners' Club. Still, we can take a tip from them. On alternate weeks (that's right, you mow *every* week during the growing season and no skipping) cut your lawn in an opposite direction—north and south, then east and west. Reason: Grass gets pushed down under mower wheels and doesn't spring up fast enough for a sharp cut. If you continually mow in only one direction, ridges of taller grass will begin to show up after a while.

ABOUT GRASS CLIPPINGS

Hook on a basket to catch clippings from a reel-type mower and attach a bag to a rotary if a blowing outlet is provided. (If not, you'll have to rake the clippings off by hand.) You may have heard that it's good to leave clippings where they fall, that they form a mulch and cool grass roots; but, even as a Lazy Gardener, you cannot listen to such siren songs. What clippings do if they're left around is rot. And rot encourages fungus. And fungus is a prospect that should make you blanch—as you'll find out later.

DICHONDRA: ODDBALL LAWN

In Southern California and a few other sections of the country, Dichondra is widely used as a lawn substitute. Or, to be fair, in *preference* to the lawn grasses available.

Dichondra is a creeping, clover-like plant which, when it grows together, creates a smooth, interestingly textured turf. It won't take frozen conditions, which limits its range. It also won't take too much traffic, which puts it out of consideration for play or recreational areas. There's a theory around that it takes less care than blade grass lawns, but that's open to question.

Maintenance rules for Dichondra are exactly the same as for grass lawns with two important exceptions:

(1) *Herbicides:* Make *sure* you buy herbicides intended for "Dichondra Only." Otherwise, instead of killing weeds in your Dichondra, you stand a good chance of killing your Dichondra and leaving the weeds in a flourishing condition.

(2) *Mowing:* Dichondra grows more slowly than lawn grasses, so doesn't need as much mowing. But people who think it never needs

to be mowed are dreamers. It responds to fertilization with surges of growth and, in time, builds up a mat like Bermuda. To keep Dichondra in bounds (and looking like anything) it should be mowed at least once a month during the growing season at a height of one inch.

Chapter 3

FERTILIZING

Now that you've mowed, the time has come to fertilize your lawn. Perhaps you're surprised that fertilization comes next in sequence. We haven't forgotten your flourishing weed crops or the bare patches, but those nuisances will have to wait. Actually they can partially vanish as problems if you fertilize next. A vigorous, well-fed turf tends to crowd out weeds and fill in vacant spaces of its own accord.

Buying fertilizer for a lawn is a bit like buying varnish for a floor. You have to calculate the area to be covered to know how much material you'll need. The parallel is far from exact, however, since a floor is usually geometric in shape while a lawn meanders.

HOW TO MEASURE YOUR LAWN

If your lawn is a square or a rectangle you're home free. Just measure any two adjacent sides to the nearest foot, multiply, and your area is neatly converted into square feet.

But if your lawn meanders (and most do) it may take a little figuring to extract its dimensions. Perhaps the simplest way is to reduce it to a series of approximate rectangles (see sketch on page 14) and add the totals.

You can use a tape or a yardstick to help you measure, or you can simply rely on your feet. The stride (from tip of toe to tip of toe) of an average size man is about three feet. If you're unsure, draw a couple of chalk marks on the pavement a yard

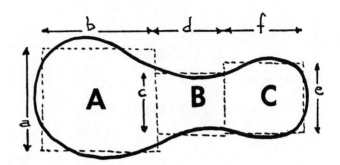

AREA OF RECTANGLE = LENGTH X WIDTH (eg: $a \times b$)
AREA OF LAWN = A + B + C

apart and check yourself out. A couple of inches either way doesn't make much difference. To all intents and purposes you're a striding yardstick.

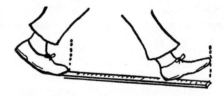

There's a final step. Having calculated the dimensions of your lawn in square feet, round off the figure to the nearest double-zero digit. Which means if you've calculated 2845 square feet, call the figure 2800 square feet. Or if you've wound up with 2775 square feet, your figure still rounds off at 2800 square feet. There's a reason for this niggling adjustment, if you'll bear with us.

Now for a real test of character. We're well aware that the last thing a bred-in-the-bone Lazy Gardener wants to do is to remember anything. But remembering the square footage of your lawn is only a little less vital than remembering your Anniversary date. If all other methods fail, you might try composing and submitting to your subconscious some little ditty such as:

My name is Jonas Cudahay.
I rise each day at dawn.
And square feet two-eight-double-ooh
Measure out my lawn.

However it's done, through poetry, astrology, numerology, or tattooing, the figure must be recorded and retained.

HOW TO BUY FERTILIZER

You arrive at your Garden Center and ask your favorite salesman for lawn fertilizer. He may not know you too well yet; he may not have plumbed the full lethargy of your lazy gardening character. You'll know if, almost automatically, he starts leading you toward the sheds where sacks of dry, bulk fertilizer are stored. Courteously but firmly you must correct his impression that you are a heaving or hauling type. What you want is liquid fertilizer— out of a bottle.*

You may almost sense your salesman's relief (he doesn't care for heaving either) as he reroutes you into the main building. (That's another plus for liquid fertilizers; they're displayed indoors, out of chill winds and hot sun.) He'll lead you up to shelves fairly bulging with bottles of various shapes and sizes. Then, if the store is busy, he may excuse himself, inviting you to make your own selection but to sing out if you're in trouble.

Your instinct will be to clutch his arm and tell him you're in trouble right now, but resist this unseemly display of emotion. In spite of unfamiliar bottles and brands, your choice isn't too hard to make. You're looking for a "straight" lawn fertilizer and the labels will inform you about the only two factors which need concern you: (1) the strength (analysis) of the fertilizer; (2) the volume of material you'll need to cover your lawn.

---

* Nine-tenths of the fertilizers sold for home lawns are in dry, bulk form, contained in sacks which weigh up to eighty pounds each. There are reasons for this but they're not Lazy Gardener reasons. Concentrated liquid materials are lighter in weight, quicker and easier to apply, and just as effective in results, if not more so.

1. The Strength (analysis) of the Fertilizer

Take down a bottle from the shelf. Examine the label and you'll see a formula of three figures separated by dashes. They may appear as 16-8-3 or 10-8-4 or 12-6-6 or in some other combination. In any case these figures represent the main chemical ingredients (analysis) of the fertilizer—nitrogen, phosphorus, potash, *always* in that order.

To simplify (even oversimplify) the action of these ingredients: nitrogen encourages top growth and is mainly responsible for "greening up" a lawn; phosphorus stimulates stem and root growth; potash also feeds stems and seems to increase the availability of other elements to the plants.

If your lawn, as a result of long neglect, is in a debilitated condition, you'll select a "strong" fertilizer (especially in respect to nitrogen) to spur your grasses into activity. Of the formulas mentioned, the 16-8-3 would seem the logical choice.

2. The Volume You'll Need to Cover Your Lawn

Now read the Instructions on the label. Perhaps they will inform you that one quart of the contents ("full strength") will fertilize 400 square feet of lawn when diluted with water. That means one gallon will cover 1600 square feet. Thus, if your name is Jonas Cudahay and you own 2,800 square feet of lawn, you'll need two gallon jars—one and three-quarters of which you'll apply, leaving a quart over.

Now you're in the position of a hunter who knows where the rabbits are and has bought the ammunition but has still no way of shooting one with the other. The analogy is reasonably exact because the missing equipment (technically a hose-end spray dispenser) is often called a lawn gun. Just to keep in the spirit of hunting, we're also going to select a pistol grip nozzle to use in conjunction with the lawn gun.

The pistol grip nozzle shown here can save you endless steps every time you attach equipment to your hose. Just make sure of one thing—that the muzzle end is threaded so a lawn gun can be screwed on.

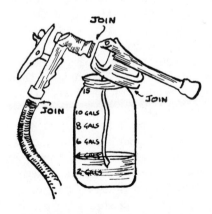

LAWN GUN ASSEMBLY: Hose, Pistol Grip Nozzle, Fertilizer Jar with Dispenser Head

You should find the lawn guns stocked close by the fertilizers. Choose one with a "fast applicating" dispenser head attached to a quart jar. This will send out a coarse spray in a hurry and cut down on the time you'll be standing around on wet grass. We illustrate the gun ready for attaching to a pistol grip nozzle and hose. (You may find it confusing that the quart jar of your lawn gun is marked in such a way as to indicate "gallons." Forget about this now. It'll all be explained later.)

HOW TO APPLY LIQUID FERTILIZER

The best time to fertilize a lawn is after a rain, or after a thorough watering which has left the ground damp but not soggy. You want the nutrients to get down to the roots as quickly as possible and damp soil acts as a conductor. So if you contemplate fertilizing during a drought (or if you live in a dry region) it's a good idea to water heavily the day before.

Read the instructions on the fertilizer bottle again carefully. Probably you'll be directed to fill your lawn gun "full strength," though the wording "apply with enough water to dilute" may appear. They both mean the same thing. Fill your quart jar to the brim with fertilizer concentrate, fit on the top, then couple up hose and pistol grip nozzle. Turn on the water at the faucet and you're ready to go to work.

You'll find, when you press the nozzle handle, that only clear water flies from the lawn gun. This situation changes when you place your finger over the "suction hole." Diluted spray now emerges at correct strength for fertilization.

Start backing across your lawn applying the liquid with a steady fanning motion of your arm. Think of it as "painting" the lawn. Try to lay down an even coat of spray across the grass. Don't worry if shrubs or flowers occasionally get splashed. They'll benefit from the extra food if rinsed off afterwards with water.

The diagram at the right illustrates a "backing path" across an irregular-shaped lawn. When you've finished one swath, back up along another, parallel to it.

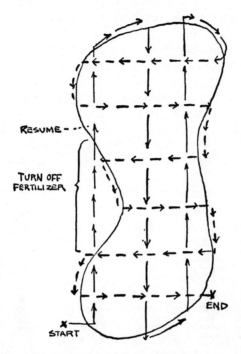

Backing path (*for lawn fertilizing*)

When you run out of fertilizer, turn off water by releasing the nozzle handle. Unscrew the quart jar and take it off the lawn for refilling. When you return, the rest of your equipment, lying on the grass, will show you exactly where to resume operations.

Gauge your fertilizer supply so that half is gone when you've covered your entire lawn with one coat. Apply the second coat criss-crossing at right angles to your former path. This pattern is important to insure even coverage and thus prevent grass from greening up in streaks.

Only apply as much fertilizer as you calculated in your original estimate. If you have a quart or so left over, resist the temptation to use it up as an extra bonus. The theory of "if little is good, more is better" just doesn't apply with fertilizers. "More" can result in nitrogen "burn"—dead leaves—from which it may take your lawn weeks to recover. Save excess fertilizer for another day.

When you've finished fertilizing, detach the lawn gun and wash the grass down with a fine spray of clear water. This will dispose of chemicals which may be sticking to the blades and nudge the nutrients down to the roots where they can do most good.

What's the time commitment in fertilizing your lawn the liquid way? Assuming you're Jonas Cudahay and that you own 2800 square feet (and have chosen a fertilizer applied at the rate of 400 square feet per quart), the breakdown is as follows:

Dispensing contents of qt. jar 7 times	
(@ 6 mins. per qt.)	42 minutes
Filling and attaching jar 7 times	
(@ 5 mins. per fill)	35 minutes
Spraying down grass and cleaning equipment	15 minutes
Total time commitment	92 minutes

An hour and a half odd doesn't seem excessive for revolutionizing the looks of 2800 square feet of grass, a lawn larger than the national average.* You can expect a surge of green (weeds included) within a few days; faster or slower depending on prevailing temperatures. Growth rates will remain high for several weeks, as you'll find when you mow. With your first fertilization you'll have taken a giant step toward converting a grass patch into a lawn.

HOW OFTEN TO FERTILIZE

They say that Green Thumbers start fertilizing at the earliest possible moment in spring and keep at it regularly every month until frost. But that's overdoing it for the undedicated. Just keep four dates in mind:

---

* Private home lawns range from front-yard postage stamps to the several acres on estates, but the fertilizer industry has come up with an "average" figure to guide it in preparing products—2500 square feet.

1. St. Patrick's Day
   (If this is unrealistic for your part of the country because of
   frosts and blizzards, either move or shift your thinking to
   April 1—April Fools' Day; or even, if you're that badly off, to
   May 1—May Day. The ground should have thawed and grass
   be sprouting as a result of seventy-degree temperatures.)
2. Memorial Day
3. Fourth of July
4. Labor Day

If you fertilize on or about those four dates it's enough to
keep your lawn flourishing. The one date about which to observe
some rigidity is Fourth of July *if* you own Bluegrass. If you miss
by more than a week, don't attempt to fertilize until the cooler
(seventy-degree) weather of September arrives. Reason: Bluegrass goes through a dormant period during the hottest months.
It stays green but can look sleepy. Growth virtually stops, as
you'll notice in mowing. Don't try to force it by fertilization at
this time. Just make sure of water and wait. Your Bluegrass will
come back strong when the children return to school.

WARM WINTER GRASSES

If you live in a frost-free region (as Chambers of Commerce
like to call them), you can continue to fertilize every couple of
months as long as your grass stays green. Bermudas, St. Augustine, and the Zoysias go brown in midwinter, but color can be
prolonged by feeding when the first fadeaway is noticed. Simi-
larly color can be brought back earlier in spring by feeding at the
first hint of green.

If you own a Bermuda, St. Augustine, or Zoysia lawn, and
don't like its midwinter "dead" look, you might try a green vegetable dye. That's what they use in football stadiums for New
Year's Day bowl games. The green isn't exactly grass green, but
it can be a bit gayer than dormant brown. Bermuda can be top-
seeded with a winter grass—Redtop is best—but St. Augustine
and Zoysia are too coarse for this treatment.

Dichondra remains green all winter but growth screeches to a halt and fertilizer won't put "go" back into its system. Nor will it help the somewhat huddled look that Dichondra leaves get in chilly weather. About all you can do is check the soil moisture and wait for spring.

LIME

Sometimes liming a lawn is confused with fertilizing it. In "sour" soils, lime can play an important part in releasing nutrients to grass roots (it neutralizes the acidity which tends to "lock up" food elements), but lime itself is not a food.

"Liming up" in spring is a widespread practice in certain sections of the country, but often it's unnecessary and wasted effort. The only way to find out in your own case is to have your soil analyzed. Fill six clean containers (empty milk cartons are fine) with samples from various parts of your lawn. In each case lift a sod and dig out earth from underneath. Fill the excavations with fresh soil before you replace the sod.

Take these samples to your Garden Center for testing (usually a free service). The results will tell you whether you have to lug and distribute heavy sacks of lime over your lawn. No Lazy Gardener wants to be committed blindly to such a fate because of some old farming tradition which may have no application to his own plot of land.

Chapter 4

IRRIGATION

In the last chapter we advised a thorough watering of your lawn prior to fertilizing if you suspected dry soil. We didn't mean to leave a false impression. Dry soil has no place under your turf at any time, and unless you counteract drought conditions on a more or less systematic basis through the growing season, you're likely to wind up wondering where your verdure went.

Since "watering" is a charged word, fraught with indignant claims and denials, let's call the deep, permeating application of moisture necessary for healthy turf by the more technical name of "irrigation."

IRRIGATION IN AREAS OF SUMMER RAINFALL

In many sections of the country spring, summer, and autumn rains provide most of the irrigation needed in a normal year. But even in the Pacific Northwest, where annual precipitation can total over a hundred inches, along comes the occasional dry spell. Grass withers and watering devices must be put to use.

Your objective is to keep grass roots growing downward as deeply as possible. When moisture is evaporated from the top layer of the soil it must be replaced. You'll know when you've accomplished this because water will back up when the soil is saturated.

Use a portable sprinkling device which delivers water slowly. A revolving jet, for instance, is preferable to a steady spray head because water has time to soak in between revolutions. Plan on leaving the sprinkler in one location until the surrounding ground is thoroughly moist (it may take an hour), then move on to the next location, overlapping slightly on the previous pattern.

Don't attempt to irrigate by a hand-held hose because:

1. It's a waste of your time.

2. You won't have the patience to stand there long enough for adequate water penetration.

3. Shallow watering may keep surface roots alive but the deep foragers will die off.

Once you've irrigated deeply you can forget about your lawn till it shows signs of wilt again. Test it with your foot. If the grass blades retain the imprint and don't spring back up, the roots are parched. Water immediately. Waiting for rain is fiddling while Rome burns.

IRRIGATION IN AREAS OF SUMMER DROUGHT

In most of the Southwest, summer rainfall is nil, or a reasonable facsimile thereof. What's more, an underlying water table is nonexistent in many areas. If you were to dig a hole in your back yard, the first time you'd observe dampness would be somewhere in the vicinity of China.

This presents a difficult irrigation problem. Every drop of water supplied to your lawn is supplied by you. And yet your grasses need the same moisture to flourish as they do anywhere else.

Under these conditions sprinklers become all important and if if you don't already possess a permanent underground system you should think about acquiring one. You can change fast from a Lazy Gardener to a full-time Water Boy if your only recourse for irrigation is hauling around hoses.

Your objective in "dry soil" irrigation is to force water down into the ground as deeply as possible. This must be done in stages. The technique is called "watering in sets."

Let's say you start with an abused lawn where water has never penetrated more than a couple of inches and your grasses are literally hanging on by their root tops. Turn on your sprinkler system and stand by. In perhaps five minutes water will be repelled by the dry soil, back up and start running off your lawn.

Turn off your sprinklers, wait half an hour, then turn them on again. It may be eight minutes this time before runoff begins.

Keep repeating this process until slowly (it may take several weeks) you can leave the sprinklers on for at least half an hour before runoff. You'll notice that your lawn has perked up as the roots move down to the new irrigation depth.

Along about now you might cut out a square of turf to find exactly how far water is penetrating. Six inches is a necessary minimum. Eight inches is good and twelve inches is excellent, especially if you're blessed with one of the heavy clay soils prevalent in the Southwest.

You can hold your moisture depth by irrigating deeply once a week. How long does it take to irrigate "deeply"? Depends on your soil. When it's saturated, water will run off.

Perhaps in very hot, dry, and windy weather you might step up the watering to twice a week if your grass shows signs of distress. But no more. Your objective is to keep the soil porous and moist, where roots can find food and air, not wringing wet where they can rot.

The best time to water is early in the morning. Reasons:

1. Grasses have all day to dry off, thus minimizing the danger of fungus diseases at night.

2. Higher water pressure (because of less competition from the neighbors).

3. Less wind to blow the water off target.

Chapter 5

WEED CONTROL

It's been estimated that out of thirty-five million home lawns in the nation, some two-thirds are infested by crabgrass. A statistic like that makes you wonder how we ever got rid of housemaid's knee because, for some time now, we've had the means to make crabgrass just as obsolete.

Crabgrass

For the benefit of the innocent and sheltered, perhaps we'd better describe what crabgrass looks like. Or is there any need? The name tells the story—an ugly, coarse, crablike growth, capable of sprawling over a square foot of ground, ripening seeds at an appalling rate.

Like any stage villain, it's a master of disguises. In spring it sprouts green, upright little shoots which hide themselves amid your choice grasses. Then, as it reveals its true crustaceous shape, it ducks low to avoid the blades of your lawn mower. By August it reaches maturity and dies, leaving its dried corpse to litter your lawn. But even after death it sneers at you, challenging you to rake out its dead thatch and plant lawn seed in the bare patch exposed. It knows that next spring its aggressive progeny will come swarming up to undo your work.

Fortunately, as we have indicated, the crabgrass reign of terror should now be history. Chemists have devised controls not only for this pest but for most other weeds which disfigure your lawn. They can be put to rout either during their active growing season, or early in spring before their seedlings have surfaced. Different poisons are employed for each purpose, known respectively as post-emergent and pre-emergent herbicides.

Post-emergent Herbicides. (*Poisons used to kill growing weeds.*) You'll appreciate that it took skilled research to develop chemicals which would hunt down and destroy crabgrass in your lawn without damaging desirable grasses. But the job's been done and discriminating, selective (and unpronounceable) substances have been bottled by manufacturers under various brand names. Since these names are not consistent throughout the country, you'd better ask your Garden Center salesman to recommend a product. If other weeds beside crabgrass agitate you, better ask him to recommend a "broad-leaved" herbicide as well.

Dandelion, clover, English Daisy, dock, and many other weeds are classified as "broad-leaved" to distinguish them from the narrow-leaved (bladed) grasses. The chemicals which work for their destruction don't mingle amicably with crabgrass-killing ingredients and fights can break out between them when locked up together in a bottle. Hence they are usually packaged and sold separately. But you can mix them in your lawn gun. In the short interval before they're shot out as spray they won't have time to squabble.

While you're at the Garden Center you might consider buying a second lawn gun for herbicide use only. It's not absolutely necessary. You can employ the same gun for all lawn purposes but, after poisons, you'd better be careful of the abandon with which you splash around fertilizers. Remnants of herbicides are hard to clean out of equipment and even small quantities can defoliate shrubs and kill flowers bordering the lawn.

We believe that the purchase of a separate gun for poisons is a wise investment. Be sure to mark it with a red sticker when you get it home, or otherwise distinguish it so you won't make mistakes.

You'll find, when you read herbicide labels, that precise measurements (in tablespoons, ounces, and cups) are called for. Unlike fertilizers, which are usually applied "full strength," herbicide instructions may read "1 cup per 5 gallons per 1000 square feet." Here's where those "gallon" markings at the side of your lawn gun jar come into play. To make up a solution sufficient for 1000 square feet of lawn, you pour one cup of the bottled concentrate into the jar and then add water up to the "5 gallon" mark.

You understand, of course, that these "gallon" markings don't represent actual volume measurements. Your entire jar, crammed full, only holds a quart. You might call them "symbolic" gallons. They become actual gallons when, mixed with hose water flowing through the head of your gun, the solution finally reaches your lawn.

Some people get irritated at chemical manufacturers because of all the pesky measurements involved in making up a herbicide solution. Why don't they prepare the stuff, as they do fertilizers, so you can apply it straight? Cost is the answer. Herbicide chemicals are expensive and water is cheap. So the manufacturers supply the essential killing ingredients and let you provide the branch. After all, unless you're a Rambling Wreck from Georgia Tech, you don't find it too arduous to dilute essential ingredients in your favorite tavern to something less than clear.

```
~❀~ LIQUID MEASURE ~❀~

3 TEASPOONS (TSP) =  1 TABLESPOON.(TBS)
2 TBS                =  1 OUNCE (OZ)
8 OZ                 =  1 CUP (C)
2 C                  =  1 PINT (PT).
2 PTS                =  1 QUART (QT)
4 QTS                =  1 GALLON (GAL)
```

MIXING HERBICIDES

Let's return to Jonas Cudahay with his 2800 square feet of greensward. If he buys a crabgrass-killing compound which calls for "1 cup per 5 gallons per 1000 square feet" and a broad-leaved herbicide calling for "3 ounces per 5 gallons per 1000 square feet," he estimates as follows:

Crabgrass killer needed for 2800 sq. ft.=2 cups 6 oz. (approx.)
Broad-leaved herbicide for 2800 sq. ft.=8 ounces (approx.)
Water needed to dilute crabgrass killer=14 gallons (approx.)
Water needed to dilute broad-leaved herbicide=Zero (the same water will serve to dilute the combined ingredients)

Obviously all this liquid is more than Jonas can fit into his quart jar at one time, so he must apply it in two batches. He'll split the ingredients down the middle, first pouring 1 cup 3 ounces of the crabgrass killer into his "Poison" jar. Next he'll pour in water, raising the level up to the "7 gallons" mark, thus insuring the correct dilution. As final steps, he'll dump in ½ cup (4 ounces) of the broad-leaved herbicide, then gently rock the jar to blend all the ingredients. Now he's ready to hitch up to his hose and pistol grip nozzle and go into action against the weeds on *half* his lawn.

APPLYING HERBICIDES

What Jonas must remember when he starts spraying is that he is dispensing far less material than when he fertilized. True, he'll only go over the area once—putting down a single "coat of paint" instead of the previous two—but even so, each partially filled jar of herbicides must get him as far as a full jar of fertilizer. Which means that he must move along at a rapid clip, barely wetting the turf as he backs across it.

The area will shrink some because he'll keep the spray carefully within the perimeter of his lawn, taking no chances of harming shrubs and flowers along the borders. But he'd be well advised to predetermine a halfway mark which must be reached before his first jar of material is exhausted—at which point he refills and finishes the treatment. If he has herbicides remaining, he can reapply it to the worst weed patches. Chances are that few desirable grasses are still in residence there, so he doesn't have much to lose by an overdose.

It goes without saying that neither Jonas—nor you—will attempt to wash off a lawn after treatment with post-emergent herbicides, since prolonged contact with the chemicals is what's going to kill the weeds. In fact, try to coordinate your spraying with a favorable weather prediction of at least forty-eight hours without rain, or you may have to douse the pests all over again. If you live in a dry region, irrigate thoroughly beforehand so you won't have to turn on the sprinklers for the next few days.

Your weeds should be withered and dry in about a week, ready for raking out—a soul-satisfying experience. In stubborn cases, where weeds are deeply entrenched, you may have to spray again after a couple of weeks, but generally one treatment is enough. You'll find yourself looking with dismay at the piebald patches where the weeds have been evicted and wondering how long before you can reseed. Don't hurry it. Postpone action until you're sure that the poisons are out of the ground. The waiting period is usually two weeks, but be guided by the instructions on the herbicide labels.

Pre-emergent Herbicides. (*Poisons used to kill seedlings before they break ground*). Applying a pre-emergent herbicide is like practicing preventive medicine. There may not be a weed in sight when you spray the chemicals on your lawn, but that's no guarantee against what may happen later unless you act in time. If crabgrass plagued you all last summer, it makes simple sense to choke off seeds before they can invade again this year. If you wait, you'll have to go after a new crop of crabgrass with a post-emergent killer which involves a lot more work.

Pre-emergent chemicals destroy weed seedlings just as they break from their shells and while still underground. They lose their effectiveness once the weed emerges into the light and begins to grow. This means that timing is all important in the use of pre-emergent compounds. You must anticipate the germination of the seeds and apply the chemicals during a brief but critical period.

When is this critical period? Early spring—whatever the month in your region. Watch your permanent lawn grasses. When they begin to green up in response to warming weather, the time has come.

You buy a bottled pre-emergent herbicide at your Garden Center and, following label directions, dilute it with water in your "Poison" lawn gun. The process is less complicated than for post-emergents since there's no mixing of chemicals designed for different jobs. Pre-emergents wipe out both crabgrass and broad-leaved weed seeds with majestic indifference.

In warm winter regions, autumn is a better time than spring for pre-emergent control. When the weather cools and rains begin, weed seeds become a menace. A treatment around Halloween should catch most of them. Follow up with an adequate fertilization program through the winter, and a spring treatment should prove unnecessary.

You can safely use pre-emergents with Dichondra. In fact, it's the best weed control possible for this type of lawn.

SPRAYING SAFETY RULES

It stands to reason that poisons which can kill plants can also do considerable damage to humans unless handled cautiously.

Never spray on a windy day—drift may get in your eyes. Early morning and late afternoon are the most likely times to find still air.

Keep your chemical bottles and spraying equipment out of the reach of children—locked up, if posssible—or on a high shelf. Make sure that children and pets are at a safe distance before you begin to spray.

Keep a separate set of measuring utensils—spoons, cups, etc.—for spray use only. Keep them securely locked away and don't let them wander back to the kitchen.

Use common sense at all times. Handle poisonous chemicals with the respect which is their due and all will be well.

RESEEDING AFTER POST-EMERGENT HERBICIDES

If you have patience there may be no need to reseed. Your basic grasses will welcome the vacancies opened up by weed removal and grow in from all sides to cover them. Still, if you've been unusually successful in your chemical kill, you may be in no mood to wait around for nature to take its leisurely course. You may want new grass to fill in those bare spots in a hurry.

First you must wait for the toxic effects to dissipate from the soil. This is usually estimated at two weeks, but let's add another to be safe. Meanwhile you can rake out the vacant areas and prepare them as seed beds, pulverizing the earth, removing sticks and debris.

When the waiting period ends, sow your lawn seed (matching it as far as possible with your existing grasses) at about the thickness used to season food with salt. Firm the soil with a board (or your foot), then water with a fine spray from your hose nozzle.

The problem now is to keep the reseeded areas constantly damp until the new shoots break ground. This is vital. If the soil dries out for even five minutes once germination begins, the seedlings and your work will be lost.

Some grasses emerge rapidly if soil, weather, and water conditions are right. Ryes and Fescues can be pushing up blades within a week to ten days. But Bluegrass may take a month. What this means is that, in hot and windy weather, somebody may have to stand by with a hose as often as six times a day to keep the seed beds damp.

Obviously this somebody isn't a Lazy Gardener. Fortunately there's a way out. You can seal off the seed beds to prevent evaporation. The materials generally used are gunny sacks, flour sacks, old sheets or shirts, any fabric which will absorb moisture. Spread these over the areas and keep them damp by a once-daily soaking. You can peep underneath from time to time to see what's doing, but don't remove the covers until a substantial stand of grass is evident. Don't worry if the new shoots look pale and sickly. They'll green up fast when exposed to light.

RESEEDING AFTER PRE-EMERGENT HERBICIDES

This isn't possible—at least for several months. The chemicals which kill weed seedlings linger in the ground and are just as toxic to germinating lawn seed.

But there should be no reason to reseed. Pre-emergents are applied to *prevent* the appearance of weeds in a reasonably healthy turf, therefore they are not responsible for bare patches which may develop later.

If your lawn is hit by fungus attacks or insect invasions during the summer, leaving denuded areas, you'd best wait till September before reseeding. The pre-emergent toxicity should have worn off by then and the cooler weather will get your new grasses off to a flying start.

Chapter 6

PEST CONTROL

BITING, SUCKING, AND CHEWING INSECTS

In most months of the growing season grubs, larvae, cutworms, and a horde of other pests can raise hob in your lawn, consuming grass blades at a rate that would make a horse look ridiculous. In a case of bad infestation an entire lawn can be wiped out.

Authorities advise keeping a sharp watch for symptoms and immediately applying the appropriate controls. This makes sense as far as authorities are concerned because it is true that certain chemicals exterminate some pests more effectively than others. But no Lazy Gardener is going to keep all that close watch for symptoms, or recognize them if he does. The first he knows is that his lawn is browning in alarming patches, at which time it's a bit late to do anything about it.

The best way to ward off unwelcome boarders is to prevent them from taking up residence. Though no single insecticide compound can put a crimp into all of the bugs all of the time, there are several excellent products on the market which can control many of them most of the time. Ask your Garden Center expert about these. Also inquire about insecticide-fertilizer combinations. The chemicals used are often compatible and so can be bottled together. Which means you can both feed your grasses and foil pests in a single operation—a chore-saving maneuver satisfying to any Lazy Gardener.

WHEN AND HOW TO APPLY PREVENTIVE PEST CONTROL

Lawn pests rarely become active till the weather warms up. Be on the alert from June onward. This conveniently coincides with your second fertilization date of the season—on or about Memorial Day (May 30).

You apply the insecticide-fertilizer combination exactly as you would straight fertilizer. You can use the same lawn gun since pesticides accidentally splashed on shrubs and flowers will do no harm. Wash off the grass afterwards with a fine spray. Though the more damaging insects feed on the surface at night—on succulent leaves and crowns—they hide underground during the day, so washing down the insecticide will deposit it in the operational area.

Unhappily some pests (leaf hoppers, thrips, others) live, eat, and breed entirely above ground. If you're invaded by these, you may have to spray a second time, using a chemical which sticks to the leaves. Consult your Garden Center salesman if necessary, but let's hope it won't be. In most years the Memorial Day treatment should provide you with reasonable protection through the summer. But take nothing for granted. If in August, when your preventive pesticide chemicals may have leached from the ground, you see moths romantically dipping and twirling at twilight above your lawn, make a mental note to head for your Garden Center next day. Poetic appearances to the contrary, those moths aren't performing a ballet. They're laying eggs and their larvae will be hatched and eating their heads off in less days than you have fingers on your two hands.

OTHER LAWN PESTS

Moles can become nuisances by tunneling under your lawn, raising ridges in drunken patterns. In our experience they're hard to catch with the usual spring traps since you have to stake out over a main tunnel to get a kill, and we always seem to pick a random alley where the little blighters never come again.

In actual fact, you should rarely be troubled by moles if you keep your lawn free of insect pests. Reason: moles are hunting for worms, grubs, and larvae for dinner and if they find the cupboard bare they'll go somewhere else.

An effective insect control program should also take care of earthworm "castings"—those little piles of unpleasantness which heap up on your lawn from time to time. Some people are enraged at the very thought of killing earthworms since they claim that they enrich and aerate the soil. There is some debate, however, whether earthworms actually do this or are only found in soil which is already enriched and porous. Unless you're passionately involved in this controversy you've nothing to lose by getting rid of earthworms and their castings.

Female dogs can be a menace to your lawn's appearance. Their strong urine chemicals burn out grass in circles. The damage is temporary but the spot is unsightly till the lawn grows back in. You can help recovery by leaching the chemicals past the roots with hose water.

Both male and female dogs can suddenly select your lawn as a public toilet area. Don't delay dealing with this because, once the word gets around, dogs can be as imitative as teenagers. Clean up the mess and powder the ground with agricultural sulfur (from your Garden Center) to dissipate the apparently hypnotic odor. Afterwards make life a living hell for any dog that even looks at your lawn. The methods are up to you.

If you live in a gopher area you can awake one morning to find yourself in serious trouble. Gophers are vegetarians and feed on tender roots and greens. They especially love Dichondra leaves and will surface in broad daylight to stuff themselves. In our experience gophers are hard to trap or poison, though some people have better luck than others. If yours runs out, we suggest you call an exterminator. He'll generally make a deal with you— so much per gopher, no scalp, no charge. But he rarely misses. Like any skilled White Hunter, he's learned to think like his quarry.

Chapter 7

DISEASE CONTROL

The microscopic organisms which attack grass plants in epidemics called "diseases" are themselves plants. But plants of a primitive, undeveloped kind. They're biologically incapable of manufacturing their own nourishment and must steal it from either living or dead food-producing plants. When they root into grass blades they consume the essential chlorophyll and the blades die.

Lawn diseases are known by different names—blights, wilts, rusts, molds, and rots—but they're all caused by some form of fungus. We should mention in passing that not all fungi are "bad." The varieties which grow into mushrooms and penicillin molds are "good" as far as people are concerned. But the forms that blotch, smear, and melt out lawns are bad news for everyone.

The reproductive parts of fungi can overwinter in your lawn. Occasionally they become active while temperatures are still low (resulting in "snow molds") but more typically they lie in wait, feeding on rotted matter, till the weather warms up. Let's call this early, inactive stage "Ground Fungus."

Fungi can live only in moisture. Generally they find conditions ideal for growth in the damp atmosphere which follows rainy spells. Then they can break from the ground and develop at astonishing speed. Their threads and spores, encompassing and consuming grass blades, spread rapidly across your lawn. Sizable areas can be wiped out in a matter of days. Let's call this second, destructive stage "Surface Fungus."

How can Surface Fungus be prevented? By holding in check Ground Fungus, killing it if possible. This can be done by combining efficient lawn hygiene with chemicals. Let's see how.

EFFICIENT LAWN HYGIENE

You can go a long way toward preventing Surface Fungus if you control three factors—moisture, grass vigor, rotting matter.

Moisture: If rain falls steadily for days, there's little you can do about turning it off. But in times of drought (or in dry climates) irrigate in the morning so your lawn can dry off before nightfall. A wet lawn at night is, for fungus, delight.

Grass Vigor: Healthy grasses resist fungal attacks; weak grasses succumb easily. Therefore a well-fed, pest-free lawn offers built-in protection. Fungus spreads fast in underfed grass.

Rotting Matter: Since fungus can exist for protracted periods in decaying vegetable matter, keep your lawn raked out and free of clippings. Also avoid mulches and manures (sometimes recommended as summer dressings) since they can cause rotting mats. Ground free of decay helps keep fungus away.

CHEMICALS

In spite of your best hygienic efforts, disease could still strike, so it's a good idea to apply a preventive chemical fungicide as an additional safety measure. The question is—when? During what month of the growing season is latent Ground Fungus likely to blossom into galloping Surface Fungus?

Golf course and bowling green superintendents are so unsure of the answer that they apply preventive chemicals every seven to ten days from March to October, a program to send shivers up the back of even the most ardent home gardener. But we, with less at stake, can afford to do some hazardous guessing. True, damp weather can occur at any time but, because of higher temperatures, it's more likely to favor fungal growth during the second half of the summer. An additional advantage to this guess is that it coincides neatly with your third fertilizing date—the Fourth of July.

Chemical Control for Ground Fungus: Lazy Gardeners will rejoice to learn that fungicides mix with fertilizers and can be bought already prepared in the same bottle. Apply the mixture exactly as you would straight fertilizer, using your lawn gun and washing off the grass blades afterwards. Your target is Ground Fungus and you hope to kill it while it's still skulking in the soil. (In a sense, you could think of the operation as a pre-emergent control.) Don't be dismayed if the fertilizer analysis reads something like 10-0-0. Nitrogen is the key ingredient in lawn feeding and applications of phosphorus and potash at other times are sufficient to maintain your grasses in healthy growth.

Chemical Control for Surface Fungus: Unfortunately, efficient hygiene and preventive chemical controls are not absolute guarantees against fungal invasion. Spores are constantly carried on the wind, or by rain, or on the feet of dogs and people. They can be carried from a neighbor's lawn to yours and, if conditions are right, take root in your grasses. Telltale signs of disease may show up a week after you've conscientiously killed your Ground Fungus.

If this happens, your only recourse is to apply a straight fungicide spray to your grass blades. This time, of course, you won't wash the solution off, since it's on the leafy parts that the damage is being done. In order to obtain maximum kill, try to time this spraying to coincide with at least forty-eight hours of dry weather.

WARM WINTER GRASSES

Warm winter grasses (Bermudas, Zoysias, St. Augustine) are not as subject to fungal diseases as cool weather, tufted grasses, but they're susceptible enough to justify the preventive fungicide-fertilizer application on the Fourth of July and a sharp lookout for trouble the rest of the year.

INSECTS—DISEASES: WHICH IS WHICH?

Both insects and fungal attacks cause grass to wither, turn off-color and die. To the expert there are differences in symptoms, but from the Lazy Gardener there is only the exasperated question: "What is it *this* time?"

Some ailments are pretty spectacular and hard to miss. The disease called Rust, for instance. Your lawn looks like a bed of rusty nails and, when you walk through it, red comes off on your shoes. Or the insect pest Sod Webworms. After they've been chewing for a while you can lift dead grass up in a mat from nonexistent roots. But most diagnoses aren't as distinct. The grass just turns yellow or brown and you know a time clock's running against its demise.

Since we've taken the position that fungal diseases become a major threat after the Fourth of July, it seems to follow that sick lawns before that date are being worked over by insects. This is generally true but there are important exceptions. Among fungi, we have already mentioned Snow Mold; there is also Melting Out, the nemesis of Kentucky Bluegrass, a disease of prolonged cool, wet weather. Among pests, there's the Japanese Beetle, who doesn't deign to visit your garden till the summer is well advanced.

So which is which? From this distance we can't say. But here are a couple of tips which may prove helpful. Browning grass in the shade, or in areas of poor air circulation, usually indicates disease. Ragged grass along the edge of your lawn may not be caused by either insects or fungi but by mollusks—slugs and snails—which emerge by night from the shrubbery to chew it. You can trace their slimy trails back to their lairs and lay poisoned bait.

If you're still in doubt (as you will be) lift a square foot of infected sod and take it to your Garden Center salesman. Diagnosis may not always be easy even for him, but at least he'll have the advantage of knowing what's making the rounds of the neighborhood.

Warning: Yellow leaves in your lawn aren't always indications of outside invaders. Check on the last time you fertilized. They could be suffering from a simple case of nitrogen lack.

Chapter 8

LAWN MAINTENANCE CALENDAR

Effective lawn care is a matter of sequence and cycle—a sequence of jobs performed during the cycle of the growing season. Let's try to sum up the phases of lawn maintenance we've discussed and relate them to the dates we've picked from the calendar.

First a word of caution. If you've entered the cycle late, don't try to catch up all at once. Activities recommended for March lose their value when attempted in August; they may even prove damaging to your lawn. There'll be another March. Meanwhile proceed along the lines indicated for the remainder of the year and plan your major campaigns for the future.

MILD SPRING CLIMATES

Date	Jobs to Be Done
St. Patrick's Day (March 17)	Feed lawn with "complete" (nitrogen, phosphorus, potash) fertilizer . . .

unless

. . . you apply a pre-emergent herbicide, in which case postpone feeding for one week.

Begin mowing as soon as your grass is up to its recommended height (Chapter 2). Continue mowing at weekly intervals throughout growing season.

After third mowing, examine your lawn for weeds. If severely infested, this is a good

Date	Jobs to Be Done
	time to apply post-emergent herbicides. Reseed three weeks later (unless earlier pre-emergent treatment makes this impossible).
	If your lawn is predominantly Kentucky Bluegrass, watch for symptoms of Melting Out (browning of lower leaves, purple spots on upper blades) in cool, wet weather. Apply fungicide promptly.
Memorial Day (May 30)	Feed lawn with a fertilizer-pesticide combination.
	Begin checking moisture content of the soil. Dry spells can start even in June.
Fourth of July	Feed and treat lawn with a fungicide-fertilizer combination.
	Keep checking moisture content of soil and irrigate when needed.
Labor Day (First Monday in September)	Feed with "complete" fertilizer . . .

unless

. . . the weather has been wet and humid through August; in which case better repeat the fungicide-fertilizer combination.

This is the best time of year to reseed all bare patches.

LATE SPRING CLIMATES

| April–May | Feed with "complete" fertilizer when grass shows first signs of green . . . |

unless

. . . you apply pre-emergent herbicide; in which case wait a week for feeding.

Date	Jobs to Be Done
	Start mowing when grass is up to recommended height.
Memorial Day (May 30)	Postpone fertilizer-pesticide application until at least four weeks have elapsed since first feeding.
	A week later apply post-emergent herbicide if weeds are a problem
	Watch for Kentucky Bluegrass fungus symptoms (Melting Out) and apply fungicide promptly.
Fourth of July	Skip the fertilizer if less than four weeks from last feeding, but spray for fungus.
	From this point on you should be in step with the "Mild Spring Climates" program.

WARM WINTER CLIMATES

Date	Jobs to Be Done
St. Patrick's Day (March 17)	Feed with "complete" fertilizer—especially Bermudas, Zoysias, and St. Augustine to speed return of color. Feed Dichondra too to force it out of its winter sleep.
	Mow dormant grasses as soon as new growth shows. Continue mowing tufted grasses.
	Apply post-emergent herbicides early in April if weeds are a problem. Reseed (or stolonize) three weeks later.
Memorial Day (May 30)	Feed lawn with a fertilizer-pesticide combination.
	Begin checking moisture. Start irrigating deeply in preparation for summer.

Date	Jobs to Be Done
Fourth of July	Feed and treat lawn with a fungicide-fertilizer combination.
Labor Day (First Monday in September)	Feed with a "complete" fertilizer. Continue to water heavily—especially Bluegrass which is waiting for cooler weather to recover from summer dormancy.
Halloween (October 31)	Apply pre-emergent herbicide if you suspect weed seed in your lawn. Follow up with a "complete" fertilizer one week later.
Thanksgiving (Last Thursday in November)	It's time to topseed Bermuda lawns (unless you used pre-emergent herbicide in October). Cut extra low (under ½ inch) and seed with Redtop or Annual Ryegrass. Top dress with a fine mulch and keep damp till seedlings appear.
From Christmas on.	Continue irrigation if rains don't come. No point in mowing Zoysias, St. Augustine, or Bermudas (unless topseeded) now. They're browned out and dormant for the winter. Bluegrass should be at its best. If growth and color flag, revive them with a straight nitrogen feeding.

Tree Maintenance

Chapter 9

THE TREE FACTORY

The last thing a Lazy Gardener wants to get entangled in is botany. He assumes that something active must be going on inside his plants to make them grow and flower and fruit, but the details seem more their business than his. Not that he's unfeeling in his attitude. He understands that plants, like people, are sometimes subject to sickness or distress and he's perfectly willing to come to the rescue with medicines, surgery, or whatever else may be required. All the plants have to do is tell him.

Unfortunately, communications between plants and Lazy Gardener can be limited unless a set of signals is set up. This requires at least a rudimentary knowledge of internal workings. Not too much. Not as much, for instance, as you need to know about what goes on inside your car. But enough so that, if a plant shivers, you protect it from cold instead of blasting it with water.

As painlessly as possible we're going to escort you on a conducted tour through a tree. We've chosen a tree rather than a pansy because it's roomier inside, though the principle of operation is very similar. We might call this a tour through a tree factory because that in effect is what a tree is. When it's running full tilt on a warm summer day its productivity can be quite astounding.

Raw materials for production—water and soluble nitrates— are absorbed underground by hair roots. They pass through the main root systems and are lifted up through the tree's trunk to the leaves. It's uncertain exactly what force lifts these columns of liquid, but up they go at about fifteen feet per hour in a large tree.

When the raw "mash" reaches the leaves, it interacts with carbon dioxide which has been drawn into the leaves from the

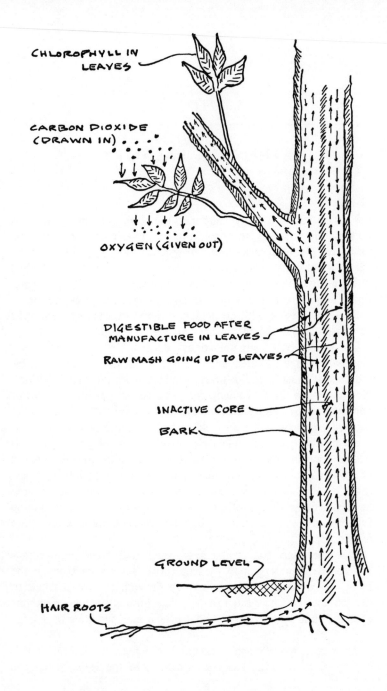

CHLOROPHYLL IN
LEAVES

CARBON DIOXIDE
(DRAWN IN) . . . .

OXYGEN (GIVEN OUT)

DIGESTIBLE FOOD AFTER
MANUFACTURE IN LEAVES

RAW MASH GOING UP TO LEAVES

INACTIVE CORE

BARK

GROUND LEVEL

HAIR ROOTS

outer air. Then the critical action takes place. In some way not completely understood, sunlight acts upon the chlorophyll (the green substance in the leaves), combining and digesting the raw materials from soil and air, transforming them into usable plant food. The process is called photosynthesis, which can be roughly translated as "manufacture through the agency of light."

The usable food (sap with a high sugar content) is now ready to circulate through the tree's system, providing nourishment to twigs, roots, bark, and branches. It can circulate immediately or it can be held in storage (in the form of starch) for hours, days, or months.

In point of fact, plant food is put to maximum use after night falls. During the day, while sunlight lasts, leaves are busy with manufacture. But in the dark hours, energy is turned toward growth. Sugar floods in to fill new cells as they elongate, divide, and subdivide at a furious rate. In certain plants at certain times of the year the speed of night growth can be phenomenal. Corn stalks in August can literally creak with surges of development.

There is an important side product to photosynthesis which is very useful for humans. Oxygen is released from the under sides of leaves. It emerges in the form of water vapor—as much as ten gallons from a large tree on a hot day. This pleasant mist serves to cool the leaves, but it also cools mad dogs, Englishmen and others who seek shelter from the midday sun.

So the next time you're tempted to ask, "What has a tree done for me lately?" here are some answers:

Trees provide unique atmosphere and setting for your home.
Large trees supply free air-conditioning in summer heat.
Tree factories manufacture pure oxygen for you to breathe while most other factories manufacture smog.

Chapter 10

TREE IDENTIFICATION AND CLASSIFICATIONS

If your trees are old familiar retainers from your grand-father's time, it doesn't much matter what you've been calling them. You know all that's important—shape, growth habit, ul-timate size—and to go poking around now into their credentials might seem an impertinence.

But if you own a newer place, and your shade trees of the future are still no more than skinny whips, it might be a good idea to check up on their potentials. People have waited years for a supposed umbrella tree to branch out, only to find that nature meant it to grow in the form of a fat cigar.

Tree identification begins with a sharp pair of hand shears. Snip off the last two feet of a leafy branch. (You still snip if it's winter and the branch is bare, but, in that case, a section of bark, hanging seed pods, and, hopefully, a photograph become ex-hibits of prime importance.) Cut off also one each of any flowers, buds, or seed clusters which may be in evidence. Wrap up these specimens in a damp newspaper and move along for similar operations on the next tree you want identified. Better call a halt after the third tree, though. There's a difference between enlightening information and total confusion.

Your friendly Garden Center expert should have no trouble naming your trees from the specimens you show him. He'll show you samples of similar types he has for sale or, if these are no bigger than your own, he may have pictures illustrating what the trees will look like when fully grown. Or he may direct you down the road to where he knows mature examples are located.

He may even suggest a visit to an arboretum. An arboretum is a kind of botanic garden where trees and shrubs are grown for exhibition and study. There are many of them throughout the country. Each state has at least one, as do most counties. The campuses of colleges and high schools can also be considered arboretums in a modest way, since they're often planted with trees popular in the neighborhood.

Viewing a prime example of your own tree may be a cause for satisfaction or dismay—satisfaction if your home-grown product conforms to the specimen, dismay if yours is runted or misshapen by comparison.

If your tree at home is still an infant, viewing its mature counterpart can also be a shock. The shock comes when you realize that a monster, capable of measuring eighty by sixty feet, is planted bang up against your living room windows. Clearly you'd better start thinking about moving the tree before you have to move the house.

We'll take up techniques for moving (transplanting) trees in a later chapter, but first we'd better inquire into growth characteristics so we don't wind up with a successful operation but a dead patient.

TREE CLASSIFICATIONS

Lazy Gardeners tend to get exasperated at trees which go bare in winter. Why do they have to act in that crazy fashion—first exploding into gaudy colors, then denuding themselves, covering the lawn with leaves? Why can't they act like Evergreens, which remain neat, coordinated, and decently clad throughout the year?

They can't because of their age-old experiences with the rigors of winter. Much as leaf-dropping trees would like to accommodate Lazy Gardeners, survival comes first.

1. Deciduous Trees (Leaf Droppers)

Deciduous trees have learned that their leaves are too many and too large to be fed during the light-shortened days and chilled temperatures of frosty weather. So they don't even try. Along about the September equinox they start sealing off food distribution and closing down their factories. Leaves, removed from the chain of supply and production, turn hues of yellow, red, and purple—color values which were recessive while green was dominant—and drop to the ground. Sap still circulates, but in reduced amounts, just enough to keep branches supple and roots alive. Otherwise the trees stand dormant, hoarding food stores, hibernating till spring.

Some of the easily recognized deciduous trees found across the continent are:

Elms
Maples
Sycamores
Ashes
Locusts
Hickories
Willows

2. *Evergreens* (*Conifers*)

Coniferous Evergreens have had a different historical experience. They found that they were able to support their leaf (needle) populations during winter because of the relatively small surface area of each unit. They also found that they *needed* their leaves to protect trunks and branches from drying winds. In extremely cold climates a snow blanket, held in place by leaves, provides additional protection. So conifer factories continue to operate through ice and sleet, but on a limited scale, with no energy expended on new growth.

Evergreens you're likely to find either as garden ornamentals or Christmas trees if you look around are:

Pines
Spruces
Firs
Hemlocks
Junipers
Yews

There are also a couple of oddities. Both Larches and Bald Cypresses are classified as Evergreens though they've lost every last leaf by Washington's Birthday. Maybe, in exasperation, he cut one of *them* down too.

3. Evergreens (Broad-leaved)

Broad-leaved Evergreens are warm winter aristocrats. Because they live in frost-free regions (or relatively so) they keep growing the year around, though less from autumn to spring because of shorter days and lower temperatures.

Among Broad-leaved Evergreens are some of the lordliest trees in the land, including:

> Magnolias
> Live Oaks
> Olives
> Camphors
> Peppers
> Jacarandas
> Citrus

Deciduous trees tend to be faster growing than Evergreens. Nothing can stop that stored-up energy which bursts out in spring and can push up six to ten feet of growth in a single season. Evergreens (both conifers and broad-leaved) grow more sedately but they liven up the winter scene with greenery and fruits.

It's interesting to note that while Broad-leaved Evergreen trees die the first winter north of their range, and coniferous Evergreens (except for locally attuned species) tend to languish away from frosts and snows, most deciduous trees flourish almost anywhere. They never overcome their suspicious attitudes, however. Bikini-clad girls may cavort on Florida beaches in January but nearby Sycamores remain totally unimpressed. Stripped for action down to the last leaf, they watch for ice storms to blow up from the equator. It could be downright embarrassing except for the reassuring presence of tropical palms and ferns.

Chapter 11

PRUNING

Let's settle one thing. Pruning doesn't "hurt" a tree in any human sense. The appearance of sap, which may follow a cut, only indicates that the food supply to that area has been interrupted. Usually the cut dries over within a few minutes as the food stream is redirected in other directions.

Trees prune themselves in nature. Lower or crowded branches which can no longer reach the light are permitted to die. In the course of time rain, wind, or the weight of snow snaps off these dead limbs. The entire process may take years in a forest, while you can see the need and perform the operation in a few minutes in your garden.

Ornamental trees are pruned for three reasons:

(a) To repair damage — Cutting off storm-broken or otherwise damaged limbs.

(b) To promote health — Thinning to permit light to enter crown; removing suckers or other undesirable growth.

(c) To control shape — Ranging from simple "topping" to elaborate exercises in the pruning art.

Since different factors enter into deciduous, broad-leaved evergreen, or coniferous tree pruning, let's consider each technique in sequence.

1. PRUNING DECIDUOUS TREES

Let's refer back to a moment of dismay you may have suffered while tree gazing, as suggested in a previous chapter. You stood in front of a prime specimen of a tree—let's call it a Silver Maple. It was lofty, noble, broad—the kind of tree that picnics could be staged under, with perfect yardarms for children's swings. But you noted with concern that *your* Silver Maple wasn't growing at all like that prototype. Yours is thin and spindly, with hardly any side branching. What can you do to change its shape?

Now actually there's no reason why your Maple has to look like any other Maple. No two trees, even of the same genus, species, and variety, ever look exactly alike in nature. But a tree of a given name does arouse certain expectations of shape and characteristics and a deviate strikes the eye as odd. For instance, a Weeping Willow is supposed to look limp and lachrymose. A Lombardy Poplar is supposed to be tall and columnar. A Texas Umbrella Tree is supposed to be shaped like a bumbershoot. An Oak is supposed to grow broad and rugged, a Birch slender and graceful—and you take it from there.

In the last analysis a tree is more valuable in dollars and cents (if you'll forgive the vulgarity) if it looks the way it's supposed to look.

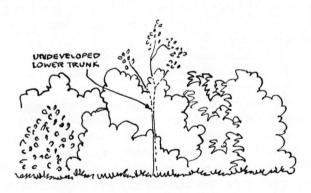

UNDEVELOPED
LOWER TRUNK

Your Maple in a crowded woodlot reaching for light

So your dissatisfaction with your spindly Maple is well founded. But before we rush forward with advice on how to change its shape through pruning, let's ask a few questions.

How did the tree get that way? Is there a physical explanation for its slender growth? For instance, could your home once have been a woodlot which was cleared for building? If so,

trees crowding around your Maple could have forced it to grow
tall, without width, to reach the light.

An examination of the tree should clear up this point. If the
side branches are now beginning to develop, since light and air
are available on all sides, this could be a possible explanation.
Top pruning will encourage side growth and help bring the tree
back to shape.

But suppose there never was a woodlot. Suppose you know
for a fact that the tree was planted six years ago by your prede-
cessor. Why has it grown straight up instead of spreading outward? Again there could be a physical explanation—deer nibbling off the side shoots, perhaps. Again we can help the tree by
top pruning to *force* side growth—making sure that, in future,
succulent new shoots are protected by wire netting.

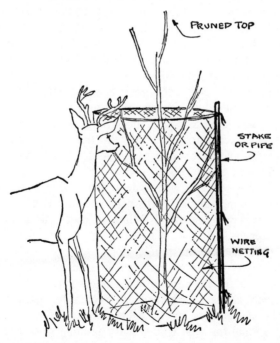

The point we're trying to make is that it's no good just whacking
away at a tree if we can't be assured of conditions which will
permit it eventually to grow into the desired shape.

We can best show the pruning required for your spindly Maple by a series of drawings. We picture the tree in midwinter (January or February) with leaves off, since that's the only time major pruning should be attempted on a deciduous tree.

To simplify our drawings we've left out a thousand small twigs which are always getting in your nose and ears when you're up a tree trying to prune. You'll have to cut out a certain number of these in the course of shaping things up. Use hand shears, long-handled loppers, or a tree saw, depending on the diameter of the branch to be cut. Treat any cut you make over half an inch in diameter with tree wound compound. This seals off the possibility of insect or fungus penetration. The compound comes in a handy-sized aerosol bomb. Whoosh, whoosh, and you're ready for the next cut.

We're reserving a discussion of the actual technique of pruning for another section of this book. (See SHRUB THINNING AND PRUNING, Chapter 17.) Just where you cut a branch, at what angle, and for what expected results are fully covered there. Shrub pruning requires a bit more finesse than tree pruning but the principles are exactly the same.

Now that you've completed your first "structure" pruning of your spindly Maple don't think you can turn your back on it yet. You'll note that in our Sketch D, much of the expected new growth will take place, crisscrossed, *inside* the tree. Make sure to cut out this twiggy mat next winter so that all food and growth energy may be directed to the outer limbs.

A final point concerns your safety. How large a pruning job should you attempt unaided? It's cold work up a tree in winter and a ladder slipping or a limb falling on your head is not funny when it happens.

As a general rule of thumb, don't attempt a pruning cut higher than you can reach comfortably from an eight-foot step ladder. And under no circumstances attempt to saw through a thick branch above your shoulder. Foolhardy risks are completely out of character for a Lazy Gardener. Hire a competent tree professional for even mildly heavy pruning work and benefit by not having to clean up afterwards.

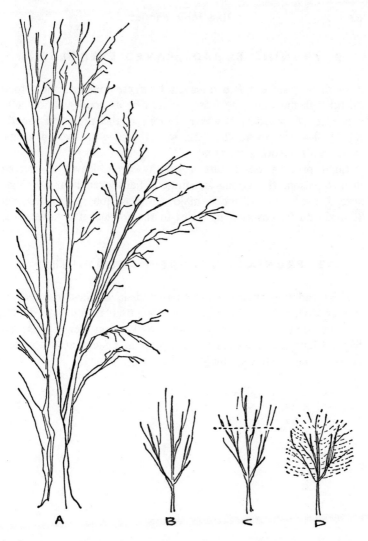

A. *Specimen Silver Maple* B. *Your Maple before pruning* C. *Your major pruning cuts* D. *Anticipated path of new growth*

2. PRUNING BROAD-LEAVED EVERGREENS

In theory, since a Broad-leaved Evergreen manufactures food all through the year, one season should be as good as another to prune it. In practice, however, March is the preferred month. This will allow you to clean out winter damage as well as shape your tree for spring growth.

Light pruning won't hurt a healthy Broad-leaved Evergreen at any season. If you can substitute a half-dozen light prunings, spread over a year, for a major surgical job, your tree will reward you by covering up holes in the foliage at a faster rate.

3. PRUNING EVERGREENS (CONIFERS)

Neat and tidy growth is as characteristic of most conifers as it is of kittens. Pines are a possible exception. If you have a Pine in your front lawn which you want to keep in sleigh bells and Santa Claus shape for Christmas, snip and snap at it to your heart's content all year long.

Chapter 12

TRANSPLANTING

Let's refer back again to your tree gazing expedition—this time to the shock you experienced when you found you had a potential monster growing bang up against your living room windows. What are your chances for moving it successfully to a more suitable location?

Pretty good, if your timing is right. It also makes a difference whether the tree is deciduous or evergreen.

1. TRANSPLANTING DECIDUOUS TREES

Let's assume that your mislocated tree is a Sycamore. You're in luck. A deciduous tree is relatively easy to transplant—if it's not too big.

What's too big? Let's put an arbitrary limit—both as to height of branches and girth of trunk. Hold a leaf rake up to the full extension of your arm. That's about twelve feet, close to maximum for a home-movable tree. Now look at the trunk at a spot about six inches from the ground. Is it thicker than the fat end of a baseball bat (2¾ inches in diameter and close to 9 inches in circumference)? It shouldn't be much thicker or you'll find yourself hoisting a good deal more weight than you've bargained for.

Our last condition is timing—time of year for transplanting. Obviously with a deciduous tree it should be early spring—before the sap starts running, as soon as you can get a shovel into the ground. This could be May in Minneapolis, March in Washington, D.C., or February in San Diego.

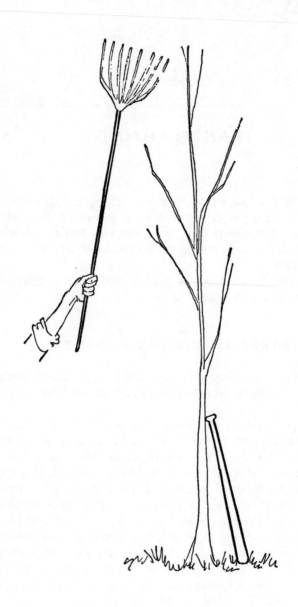

Next step is to dig up the roots, or enough of them to insure the tree's survival. Mentally (or with the point of your shovel) describe a circle on the ground tracing the path of cut you're going to make. A rule of thumb is six inches of radius for each inch of trunk diameter. Thus, for a 2½-inch diameter tree, the cutting circle would be 2½ feet wide, or approximately the size of a hula hoop.

Having described your circle, start cutting. Drive your shovel around the perimeter, slicing through roots. Keep cutting into the slit you've made, driving the shovel farther and farther toward the center, until the mass of roots comes free and the tree rocks in its basin. Your transplant is now "root balled" and ready for moving.

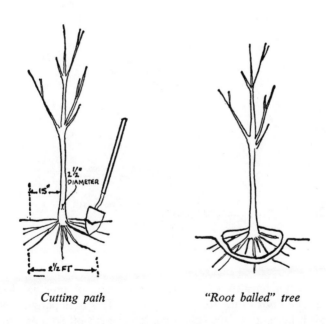

Cutting path   *"Root balled" tree*

Presumably you have long since decided on a new planting location and a new hole is ready. It should be at least a full shovel head wider than the freshly exhumed root ball and a half shovel head deeper.

Now to transfer your tree from one hole to the other. This can be the most strenuous phase of the operation, since damp earth and roots can weigh a ton. A stout tarpaulin is an invaluable aid. Transfer the tree from its hole to the tarpaulin; then, with all the assistance you can muster from your family, carry the loaded stretcher carefully to its destination.

Transfer your tree from the tarp to its new home. Shovel good topsoil under and around the root ball until it's raised about three inches above the surrounding ground level. This will allow for "sinkage" as the earth settles. Firm all loose soil in place with your foot and use excess soil to build a basin around the area. Fill this basin with water several times, till bubbles cease to come up.

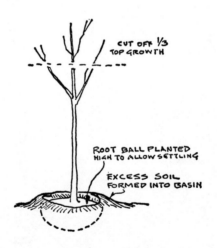

You're not finished yet. With a sharp pair of pruning shears cut off *one-third* of the tree's top growth. This is important, even though it hurts to see the height go. You've cut off so many roots in transplanting that you must compensate by cutting off top growth too.

Of course, it's entirely possible to top-prune your tree earlier, even before digging, in order to lighten the load; this is advisable if the tree is extra large or top-heavy. But usually the drastic surgery is reluctantly postponed to the end. A single season should restore most of that lopped-off growth if you make sure of ample water through the summer.

Planting a New Deciduous Tree

Suppose you decide not to transplant your own tree. You dislike Sycamores and you want to get rid of it. You've heard good things about Ashes and want to buy one. Is it harder to plant a new tree?

It's easier. You don't have to dig up an old tree for one thing. Your Garden Center will have rows of Ashes lined up, ready for you to choose from. Some may be quite big, though it's a good idea to stay within the twelve-foot limit we recommended earlier. A larger tree can go into shock and recovery may be slow.

"Bare root" tree

In spring, deciduous trees are usually sold "bare root." This means that all the soil has been washed off to facilitate shipment. It also makes the tree considerably lighter for you to handle. It's important, however, to keep the root fibers constantly damp till they're safely underground in your garden.

You take a bare root tree home and plant it exactly as you would your own transplant. Again you cut off one-third of the top (or ask them to do it for you at the Garden Center). The one new factor is staking, since a bare root doesn't have a heavy ball of soil to support the trunk and branches against winds. Drive a substantial wooden stake (or galvanized pipe) to at least two feet below soil level. Make sure it's firm, so it will be supporting the tree and not vice versa. Tie the trunk in close with plastic ribbons or strips of tire tubing. Avoid like poison any tie with wire in it because wire *is* poison. It can strangle your tree if you forget to unfasten it later.

Some gardeners find it beneficial to shake their fists at a newly planted tree and command it to grow. Lovely ladies have been known to kiss the trunk in the hope of stimulating juices. These gestures are certainly dramatic and, for all we know, helpful in getting the tree off to a good start.

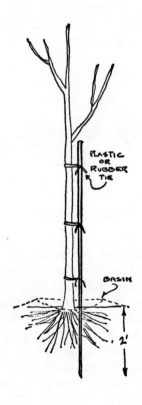

2. TRANSPLANTING EVERGREENS (CONIFERS AND BROAD-LEAVED)

Evergreens can't be transplanted as readily as deciduous trees. Since they have no true dormant period, cutting into their roots always presents hazards. It can be done—Evergreens can be successfully moved in one transplanting maneuver if great care is exercised. But it may be months, even years, before they recover from shock and look like their old selves again.

Shock can be minimized by making preparations well in advance. If you contemplate a transplant early in spring (probably the best time for all trees), begin root pruning the previous August.

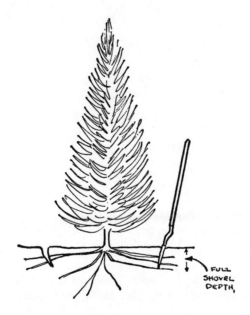

AUGUST: Root pruning
(slicing through top roots)

Root pruning is a technique for confining root growth to a limited area around the tree's trunk. The sketches show you how it's done and the results achieved. Use the same calculations as before for describing a circle—six inches of radius for each inch of trunk diameter. For the August pruning slice around this circle, driving your shovel down to its full depth.

Do nothing more till October, or just before hard frost. Then drive your shovel around the perimeter again, cutting off roots which have developed since August.

OCTOBER: Root pruning
(*keeping top roots confined in thick mat*)

In spring comes the big push. Complete digging out the root ball and carefully, *very* carefully, move your plant to its new location.

Under this treatment your Evergreen should suffer from little or no evidence of transplant shock. The lower roots may be

DIG TRENCH
AROUND PERIMETER

LINE OF
CUT FOR ROOTBALL

SPRING: Transplanting

bruised by the final surgery, but the undisturbed mat of top roots should immediately establish a feeding system to start the tree growing. Just make sure of adequate water during the first full season.

Planting a New Evergreen Tree

Evergreens* are packaged and sold at most seasons of the year in one of two ways, depending on custom in different parts of the country.

Balled-and-burlapped—meaning they've been root pruned in the field over a period of time, then dug and placed on burlap which is tightly wrapped around the root balls, or

Container Grown—meaning plants which have spent their lives confined in cans or boxes.

You plant balled-and-burlapped (B & B) trees just as they

---

* Also deciduous tree after the spring "bare root" season is over.

come from the Garden Center, sack and all. Don't try to remove the burlap or you risk damaging fine hair roots. The roots will grow through the material without any trouble and the cloth will rot away in time.

Boxes and cans must be removed from container-grown trees before planting. Ask your Garden Center friend to slit cans for you before taking the plants home. He has professional shears which make short work of the chore. If for some reason you're stuck with it, use tin snips. Never try to pull a plant out of an uncut can. It's guaranteed to break the root ball. If a tree is boxed, dig a big enough hole to receive box and all, then break off the wood with a hammer.

It isn't necessary to prune the top of a B & B or container-grown tree after planting, though you may want to do some cutting for shape or to remove broken branches.

What's the maximum size of Evergreen you should attempt to move in your garden, either through transplant or purchase? Height indications are unreliable since evergreen growth rates vary so much, but we come back to our old stand-by—the fat end of a baseball bat—as the outer limit of trunk size.

This is not to say that larger Evergreens can't be moved. Sixty-foot-high Pines and forty-foot-wide Magnolias are routine transplants for contractors with special digging and lifting equipment. When Disneyland in California was landscaped, spikes were driven through enormous Olive trees so they could be swung up in the air by cranes. Leaves and root balls were kept damp by continuous artificial mist as the trees were trucked a hundred miles to their destination. They were planted with hardly a missed beat in food production and digestion.

But such spectacular achievements are somewhat removed from the man with the hoe—or whatever implement you favor for transplanting. In the long run it's more practical to move trees with trunks no wider than the fat end of a baseball bat and let them grow into giants later.

Chapter 13

TREE FERTILIZING—DISEASES AND PESTS

Few people give a thought to fertilizing a mature tree and there's seldom any reason why they should. It's seemingly the most stable unit in your garden, self-supporting, undemanding. But there are two periods in a tree's life when your special attention can pay dividends—when it's very young and when it's very old.

FERTILIZING YOUNG TREES

We've discussed in the previous chapter the planting and transplanting of young trees in early spring. Their first season of growth is critical and a fertilization program should be considered. If all goes well, if new leaves and stems of healthy color appear when the weather warms up, they'll benefit from a first feeding on or about July 4 and a booster supplement some six weeks later.*

The fertilizer to use is blood meal. This is a dry, granular substance, purchasable at your Garden Center in ten-pound packages. It's an "organic" fertilizer, which means that it derives from a natural source and therefore is less likely to "burn" delicate roots than chemicals. Blood meal analyzes at 13-0-0, which means it's all nitrogen, stimulator of top growth. It also has the advan-

---

* If all is *not* well, if the tree lags, don't fertilize. Continue watering and hope for the best. The Golden Rule is:
      "Feed a plant that's looking fine,
      Never one that's in decline."

tage of releasing its nutrients slowly, thus feeding roots at a steady rate rather than on the "shot in the arm" principle.

You apply the blood meal by sprinkling a couple of handfuls around the outer edge of the water basin, then flooding with the hose to soak down the red substance.

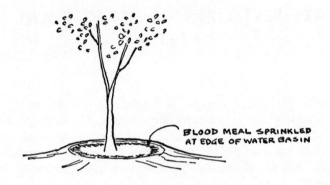

BLOOD MEAL SPRINKLED AT EDGE OF WATER BASIN

You should see results by the end of July, a new surge of green growth. Fertilize again in mid-August. After that you can consider your duty to your new tree done for the season.

FERTILIZING OLD TREES

An old tree, full of years and character, may start to lose vigor. Leaves will become sparse, new shoots may fail to appear. What could be happening is that roots are dying off as food sources become exhausted.

There's a lot of life left in many an old tree if you want to make a fight for it. Since its roots go deep you'll have to buy a root feeder to reach them. The instrument looks like an outsized needle which pushes two feet into the ground. A food cartridge is placed in the head. Water from your hose, playing over the cartridge, dissolves it slowly, thus seeping nutrients deeply into the soil.

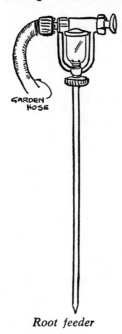

GARDEN
HOSE

Root feeder

The root feeder should be pushed down at various stations along the tree's "drip line." As shown in the sketch, this is the theoretical line where rain, sliding off the tree as if from an umbrella, falls to the ground. It's a circle around which the majority of a tree's feeder roots concentrate.

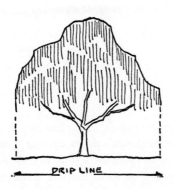

DRIP LINE

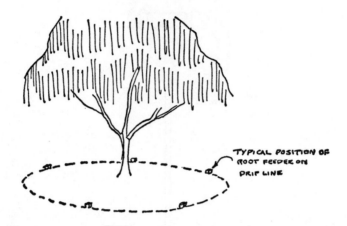

TYPICAL POSITION OF
ROOT FEEDER ON
DRIP LINE

Let the hose water trickle slowly over the food cartridge. Every half hour or so move the root feeder to a new position along the drip line. When you've traversed the perimeter, the cartridge should be exhausted, the tree well fed and, incidentally, handsomely watered.

Repeat the feeding every six weeks until the tree returns to health. If you succeed in restoring its vitality, you'll have the satisfaction of knowing that you've gained perhaps fifty years of mature dignity on any tree you might have planted in its place.

DISEASES

Ordinary fungal diseases are not a serious threat to your trees—certainly nothing in comparison to the epidemics which can sweep your lawn. Air circulation is the difference. Trees (also shrubs and vines) stand up to the breezes. Lawn grasses huddle on the ground, crowded and compressed. Still, as the old farmer said, there's one for everything, and trees are no exception.

Tree leaves are occasionally blotched by fungal blights and mildews, but most such afflictions can be (and usually are) safely ignored. If more dramatic symptoms show—defoliation or die-back of branches—you must suspect a bacterial or viral disease. Either sickness is too complicated for home remedies. If the tree is worth saving, ask your Garden Center salesman to recommend a competent tree specialist.

PESTS

Most chewing and sucking insects can find more succulent fare than leathery tree leaves. Certainly mature trees are rarely troubled by leaf eaters, though they can be invaded by borers. These tough snouted pests drill through bark and into trunks, constructing homes. Fresh sawdust is evidence that they're at work. An ordinary household insect spray should discourage them, though you may have to keep at it all summer to evict them permanently.

Undoubtedly the most conspicuous tree marauders in many sections of the country are tent caterpillars. They begin depredations in early spring and, because of flamboyant life styles, arouse particular ire among home owners.

Their barracks are easy to spot. They look like cones of white hospital gauze wrapped around the forks of still leafless trees. Inside this shelter, T. Caterpillar and about a million relatives squirm around waiting for foliage to appear. At which point they shuffle out, cafeteria style, and gobble it off.

The old way of handling this menace was to make torches of rolled newspapers and attempt to burn the tents. This was pretty spectacular and a good time was had by all, except that you probably did more harm to the tree by scorching its bark than the caterpillars would have done by eating its leaves. Not to mention scorched hands and clothes and the occasional head of hair that went up in smoke.

The method recommended nowadays is to break up the tents with a rake and spray the raggedy rubble with insecticide. You may have to repeat the attack on some double-ply, hemstitched tents but total victory should be yours in a couple of campaigns.

Nothing is more elevating to the spirit of a Lazy Gardener than to triumph over a *seen* enemy for a change—after all those battles with invisible lawn pests.

Chapter 14

FRUIT TREES AND PALMS

DECIDUOUS FRUIT TREES

If you own deciduous fruit trees we must assume that you inherited them with your homestead. Or possibly you purchased them during some misguided period before you became aware of this book. Because if there's ever a moment when a self-respecting Lazy Gardener starts down the mad toboggan to abject horticultural drudgery, it's when he first seriously contemplates raising fruit for *fun.*

To produce sweet, succulent, edible fruit there can be no compromise with work. You have to be eternally at it—pruning, thinning, spraying, cultivating, fertilizing, cleaning up windfalls, fighting off marauders—if you hope to wind up with anything but misshapen, core-rotten culls.

Why?

Let's return to our concept of the tree factory. We have seen the efficiency with which food is produced. But food is only a means to an end. The ultimate and climactic goal, to which all others are subordinated, is the production of seeds. Seeds are a tree's children, its heirs to perpetuate the race. The very existence of a species depends on producing offspring in vast quantities, since only a few can survive in the fierce competition of nature.

Through thousands of years plants have developed ingenious stratagems for protecting and distributing their progeny. There are seeds equipped with wings which fly through the air, and seeds which explode out of pods, hopefully to land on uncluttered soil where they can take root and grow. Some seeds are covered with burs which catch on the coats of animals and so are carried for miles before being scratched off. There are seeds which won't germinate unless scorched by fire, thus insuring light and air and fertilizing ashes when the blaze subsides and the young plants emerge. If this means a wait of a hundred years, that's nothing to the longevity built into other seeds. Maybe you don't fall for tall tales of sprouting grains taken from the tombs of the Pharaohs. (The desert air would long since have dried them lifeless even under tomb conditions.) But viable seeds of the lotus, authenticated as a thousand years old, have been found in the peat bogs of China. There are seeds which refuse to sprout unless passed through the digestive tracts of birds, and there are seeds with such tough casings that they can drift for years on rivers and oceans seeking habitation on distant shores.

But the most Machiavellian of all seed packages is the soft, sweet, succulent pulp of fruit. The biological intention is that animals will convey the juicy morsels to some open glade, consume the flesh and bury the seeds for winter forage. Overlooked and forgotten seeds will germinate and emerge in spring under ideal conditions. If birds attack the fruit, it works out equally well. Smaller seeds are swallowed whole and deposited elsewhere, wrapped in neat fertilizer packages. Larger stones are knocked down with the fruit, to be covered by rotting pulp.

What this means is that you are in active competition with every pestiferous varmint in the neighborhood for *your* orchard products. And we haven't even mentioned hordes of creeping, crawling, and flying insects which are also fruit lovers.

Of course, despite these concerted attacks, it's still possible to produce respectable table fruits, but you're not going to find out how here. You're only masquerading as a Lazy Gardener if the grim prospect challenges instead of revolts you. (Commercial growers spray from twelve to sixteen times a season to produce apples for the market—a statistic which should flatten any faint hope you might have that we're only kidding.) The next time you're overcome with a yearning for products of deciduous fruit trees—apples, figs, plums, pears, peaches, apricots, nectarines, or whatever—we suggest you head for the Supermarket instead of your Garden Center.

EVERGREEN FRUIT TREES

Having thrown the book at deciduous fruits, we hasten to praise the products of Broad-leaved Evergreens. If you live in a region where citrus, avocados, or mangoes can be grown, you're in luck. The trees are handsome, the fruits are delicious and can be produced with very little effort since they attract few pests.

Somehow nature slipped up on seed distribution methodology with Evergreen fruits. Juices are manufactured on the acid side, unappealing to sweet-toothed wildlife. Just us humans like them. If nature meant *us* to serve her purpose by going around spitting seeds into vacant lots, she slipped up there too, fighting a losing battle with Emily Post.

PALMS

Palms too can classify as fruit trees. In sections of California, where it's so hot that water boils in swimming pools, dates are big business. And there are regions in Florida where, at certain seasons, you must look sharp to keep from being conked by coconuts. But in both states, and a few other favored localities, Palms are generally thought of as ornamentals and their incidental fruits as nuisances.

Palms aren't really trees. They're more closely related to grasses and bamboos than Oaks and Sycamores. They don't have bark on trunks and branches. They don't even have branches—but who's to quibble? They shoot out handsome, arching leaves which *look* like branches and make Palms look enough like trees to be called trees.

In warm winter climates, Palms make a distinctive contribution to the landscape. They're especially useful around pools because they provide tropical atmosphere and don't shed leaves.

Palms are classified as either Fan Palms or Feather Palms. Those extra tall types which dominate the sky line of Southern California are Mexican Fan Palms. The characteristic species in Florida is the Royal Palm, feather leaved. Both are sun-loving plants but there are many delicate Palms which prefer shade.

We have said that Palms don't shed leaves. Their leaves die—

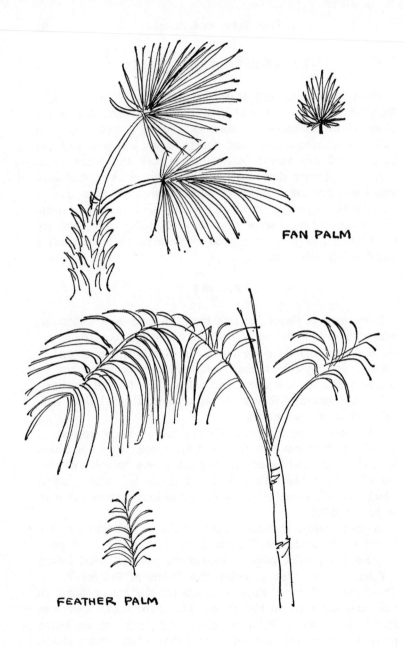

FAN PALM

FEATHER PALM

at about the rate new ones are formed—but, with some exceptions, they don't drop of their own accord. They cling to the tree until you remove them, which can cause problems when your Palm grows beyond reach of your ladder. It doesn't disturb a Palm to wear a skirt of dead leaves under its head, but it disturbs many Palm owners who consider the sight indecorous. About the only solution is to hire a professional with a power hoist. He sits in a bosun's chair a hundred feet up and saws away merrily.

Palms are easy to transplant (even big ones) because of the amazing regenerative ability of their roots. Midsummer is the time to move them, the hotter the better. They may lose every leaf in the first few weeks but new fronds come along with a rush.

Palms are accommodating about water; they can get by on very little or thrive on a lot. The old Bedouins, who were experts on Palms because they depended on dates to break the monotony of goat stews, used to say that a Palm likes its head in the sun and its feet in water. It has been estimated that a large Palm can transpire (release through its leaves) a hundred gallons of water vapor during a single hot day.

If you live in a cold winter climate you may feel that Palms are only for movie stars and sun-baked senior citizens, but this isn't necessarily so. We're willing to wager that Palms are featured in the lobbies of your best hotels, and very probably in your airport and bus station as well. Potted Palms, it is true, but they are no less decorative for being confined. Many Palms are easy to take care of indoors. Among those most frequently seen are:

Neanthe Bellas
Fish-tailed Palms
Lady Palms
Sago Palms
Kentias

All these Palms are relatively slow growing and will remain handsome in your home for years. Water them once a week (make sure of drainage) and fertilize them once a month with a recommended houseplant food.

You needn't worry about winter temperatures. If your house is warm enough for you, it's warm enough for your Palms. In summer (after night temperatures reach forty-five degrees) take them out to your patio, or plunge the pots into the soil in shady areas near your front doorstep. You'll be delighted at the "tropical" atmosphere they'll lend to your home, if only for a few months.

Shrub Maintenance

Chapter 15

SHRUBS AND THEIR PURPOSE

Suppose you're a shrub.

Suppose you're a Forsythia planted in front of a nice home. It's early spring and your branches, loaded with yellow blossoms, provide the only color in a still bleak landscape.

Your owners are proud of you. They smile at you frequently and bring the neighbors over to show you off. And indeed you're a beautiful sight as you nestle against the house blooming your head off. You're four feet high, just flush with the living room windows, and four feet wide, just touching the chimney.

Only one thing mars your happiness. You know that as your blossoms fade your owners are likely to turn their fickle attentions elsewhere. You brood over this and come up with a scheme of action which should hold their interest all season long.

You decide to *grow*—not just ordinary growth, but at a rate that will be truly astonishing. It's tough to scrounge food and water in competition with tree roots which have invaded your area, but you struggle valiantly and by midsummer develop three feet of arching growth. It's a disappointment that your owners don't notice, but you keep right on growing, knowing it'll be a different story next spring.

Spring comes and you blossom out in full glory. But instead of smiling, your owners frown. They complain you're blocking the view from the living room windows and your side branches are halfway across the chimney. Out come the pruning shears and off comes most of your new growth.

What's to be learned from this moving little epic?

First, it demonstrates the predicament shrubs find themselves in. Caught halfway between trees and lowly flowers in growth habits, they hardly know what's expected of them unless firmly guided.

Second, it serves to warn Lazy Gardeners. Beware of planting innocent-looking little shrubs too close to your doorway. You may have to fight your way past them in a couple of years with a machete.

Moral: Inside every shrub there's a tree struggling to get out.

THE FUNCTION OF SHRUBS

If you live in an old home, chances are that you've come to think of your shrub plantings as hostile, invading jungles. Periodically they must be lopped, topped, even felled to the ground, to keep them under control.

Even if you live in a newer home, where massed growth isn't yet overpowering, you may still occasionally wonder just what shrubs are supposed to *do*. There's no doubt in your mind what trees are supposed to do. They provide shade and upright accents which complement the house. Lawns provide restful greenery and open up the yard. Flowers look pretty. But just how do shrubs fit in?

Sometimes their function is obvious. A shrub which scrambles up a blank wall, facing it with graceful patterns, is both useful and decorative. So are well-located flowering shrubs, and screening shrubs which block out unsightly vistas. And nobody debates the value of a clipped hedge serving as a boundary.

But what about that snarled mass of shrubbery which chokes the windows and walls of many homes? What's the justification for it?

In most cases, not much.

Foundation planting today is usually archaic—a tradition perpetuated from another era. Back in the time of coal cellars and poor cement, foundation planting served a useful purpose. It covered the joint between protruding cellar walls and the sideboards of the house. Now such construction is obsolete. Modern concrete is impervious to water seepage and cellars are driven down where they belong—below the ground. Often the cellar is

eliminated altogether, since modern heating methods make
bulky furnaces unnecessary.

Still the foundation planting tradition persists long after the
need for it has gone. It's like the cuffs on men's pants, rolled up
to let you cross a muddy street without splashing. Or the engine
in front of your car, located where old Dobbin used to pull the
buggy. A fashion, once established, dies hard.

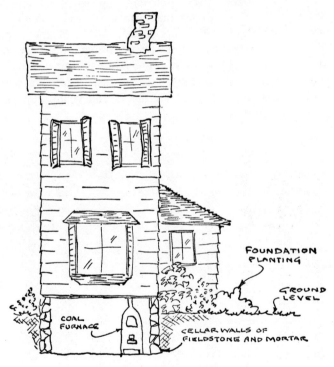

Foundation planting was useful once.

There's another holdover we ought to look into briefly—shrub
borders. They hark back to the period of the great estates. If
you happened to own a mansion set on a hill and overlooking a
rolling lawn of several acres, it made sense to border your property with a mass of shrubs as a transition from cultivated garden
to the wilds. But in a suburb there are no wilds, and shrub

borders, which are planted regularly as clockwork, simply take up room which could be better used for something else.

Our message is that you don't need to be bound by the past. Shrubs can and should be important in your garden, but the old-fashioned practice of planting mixed varieties, helter-skelter, up against the house or along the property line, is kaput. Massed shrubs, when set out today, should be selected for texture, color, uniformity, and orderly growth, qualities emphasized by repetitive patterns. This is not to say that plants of unique character or blossoming habits are to be neglected. They become more valuable than ever when treated as star performers, highlights of the garden design, not ciphers lost in the shrubbery jungle.

Later we'll have more to say about the uses and abuses of shrubs, but first we'd better learn the names and values of those already in your garden.

Chapter 16

SHRUB IDENTIFICATION

Let's assume it's late spring so your shrubs are in leaf and possibly in flower. As with tree identification, you cut off branches (with blossoms, if any) and wrap each set of specimens separately in damp newspaper. Since you probably have a much greater variety of shrubs than you had of trees, it might be a good idea to sketch out a plan on paper showing the location of each plant in relation to the house. Draw a circle for each shrub. Later, when identification is made, the appropriate name can be filled in.

You may find that your Garden Center salesman throws you some unexpected curves when he starts naming your specimens. He may identify some by difficult-sounding Latin words, and even your jovial inquiries as to "What's that in English?" won't help him elucidate if a plant doesn't possess a common name.

In the course of time, and despite the frowns of systematic botanists, most familiar shrubs have acquired descriptive nicknames, bestowed upon them by affectionate gardeners. *Kolkwitzia amabilis* has become Beauty Bush, *Spirea prunifolia* Bridal Wreath, and *Hibiscus syriacus* Rose of Sharon. Nobody outside a Botany Department would dream of calling them anything else. But with *Xylosma congestum,* to give one instance, the friendly name pattern breaks down. For some reason, no one's come up with an everyday substitute for this jawbreaker (pronounced "Zylosma," to compound the felony) so you're stuck with either calling it "that plant" or making a conscientious effort to learn the botanical name. The latter course seems best, and usually it's not that difficult. After all, you've probably mastered "Cotoneaster" since overcoming an early tendency to call it Cotton-easter, and "Euonymous" no longer holds terrors since you plunged into it

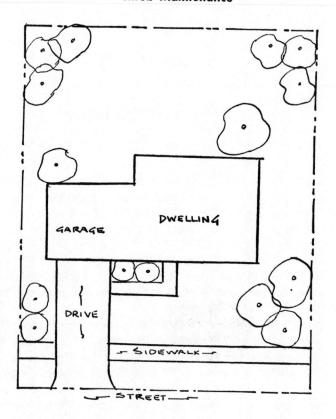

Plan showing existing shrubs

with a "You." Even "Rhododendron" hardly falls trippingly from the tongue, except you're so used to it by now.

After your Garden Center friend has identified your shrubs, wander through his nursery rows for a bit, examining similar plants offered for sale. You may be surprised at what you'll learn. Some dismal flop-head at home may turn out to be a traffic stopper when you see it growing under prime conditions.

Also note the sun and shade requirements of different shrubs. You'll see that some are kept out in the full heat of day, while others are drawn in under lath canopies or placed in the shade of trees. Shrubs can be demanding about location. Sun-lovers tend to grow limp and leggy in the shade, while shade-lovers turn miserable hues of yellow and brown in the sun. It could be that some indifferent performers among your shrubs at home are suffering from poor "exposure" (location in respect to the sun).

Another rewarding aspect of your Garden Center tour will be to "get your eye in" on the appearance and characteristics of plants which interest you. Once you're sure of a Japanese Andromeda, for instance, you'll recognize another whenever you see it—whether growing in a front yard as a rounded shrub, pruned as an espalier, or masquerading in old age as a small tree. You can get ideas from these observations. It may mean the difference between digging out an ungainly plant you own at home or, with a fresh eye for possibilities, training it for a new destiny.

Finally, your inspection circuit will introduce you to novel and appealing shrubs you may want to experiment with some day. But don't be in a hurry about this. Wait till you see how the plants develop when growing in someone else's garden. Shrubs, bought on impulse like women's hats, don't often pay off as you'd hoped.

Chapter 17

SHRUB THINNING AND PRUNING

THINNING

We're going to assume that you own an older home and that foundation planting is garroting your walls while shrub borders are cluttering your boundaries. If you are a new home owner, and these are not your present problems, take warning of what may happen in a few years.

We start our inspection trip around your house with a coldly critical eye and only one criterion in mind. Each shrub or group of shrubs crowding the building must perform some useful function in order to be worth retaining.

Usefulness can have many meanings. A lacy shrub which covers a kitchen window and keeps the sun out of the cook's eyes is useful. So is a low-growing Evergreen which camouflages a gas meter. A Holly which provides boughs and berries at Christmas is superbly useful. So is a flowering plant which doesn't camouflage anything or provide anything beyond being beautiful in blossom.

You see the principle. You want to keep whatever has value but dispose of clutter. Shrubs which are all stem and no leaf are clutter. So are shrubs which have developed into thickets, dampening walls and darkening windows. Shrubs which, through constant hacking, look as though they'd grown under a grand piano are clutter with a vengeance.

*Un*clutter, but with a watchful eye. Clean out the undesirables one by one, studying the effect after each removal. You might change your mind about some plants as deforestation progresses.

For instance, you might suddenly remember that a tall, gangling shrub gives you a cheerful glimpse of leaves at your bedroom window when you first open your eyes in the morning. Pruning can encourage its tree-like growth, so save it.

Shrubs you remove should be disposed of completely and finally. It's no good just cutting them off at the base. Suckers will appear within weeks and the plant will resurrect itself denser than ever. Uprooting a shrub, if it can be done without too much effort, is still the best method for removal. But if trunks and stems are thick and tough, you can cut them to the ground and paint the stumps with 2-4-D.

2-4-D is a liquid chemical which can be purchased at your Garden Center packaged under various trade labels. It's a "systemic," which means that it's drawn through the plant's root system, killing as it goes. It's manufactured primarily as a weed herbicide, for which purpose it must be considerably diluted with water. But it also can be applied "full strength" to spell a final requiem for stumps. It's dangerous though, so read the directions carefully.

We've found that a cotton swab on a stick (called "throat swabs" at drug stores) is the easiest and safest way to apply 2-4-D. It keeps your fingers in the clear as you paint the chemical on the stump, and the swabs can be disposed of afterwards in some child-proof place. An important feature of 2-4-D is that it won't damage roots of surrounding plants—unless in the very unlikely event of a natural graft underground.

A single application should finish off most stumps. Occasionally a few suckers may subsequently appear, but drops of chemical on their leaves should provide the *coup de grâce*. Stumps and roots can be left in the ground to rot.

Having thinned out around your house, let's turn our attention to your shrub borders. Your perspective will be different here— in many ways the opposite of your attack on foundation planting. On your property line, overgrown shrubs tend to be valuable if they provide screening. A tall Viburnum which hides a telephone pole, a fat Spirea which blocks off the gas works, a wide Mock Orange which stands between you and your neighbor's unmentionables on wash day are all friends of the family. Anything that sprawls, climbs, or tangles—eating up valuable space without utilitarian or ornamental returns—is clutter and should be given short shrift.

When your cleanout is completed, the results should be quite striking. You'll be conscious of light and air as never before, and you may even find that you are actually seeing your house fully for the first time.

PRUNING

Pruning is a dramatic and, to some people, inscrutable art. Through pruning, a shrub (or tree) can be forced to grow shorter or taller, narrower or broader, denser or lacier. Pruning offers the only opportunity for man—even Lazy Gardening man—to share equally with rain, sun, and the other elements in controlling the destiny of plants, and the Godlike role is extremely satisfying.

Let's see exactly what takes place inside a plant when a pruning cut is made.

We know (from our chapter called "The Tree Factory") that food is constantly circulating within stems and branches during the growing season. When a twig is cut off, an avenue of food distribution is cut off. More food is thus made available to nearby twigs, which respond by growing at an increased rate.

This principle of "redirected food" is the basis of scientific pruning. If a plant is considered too tall and slender, upright-growing branches are cut from its crown, thus forcing the development of sideways-growing branches through increased food supplies. If a plant is thought too low and squat, sideways-growing branches are cut, forcing vertical branches to assume the burden of growth. Through patient and persistent pruning, growth may be controlled in any direction and a plant trained in almost any shape a pruner desires.

Specialists in a pruning art known as topiary have converted shrubs into dogs, cats, peacocks, owls, and grizzly bears. In a routine way, they shape and market shrubs by the thousands in the form of cones, boxes, pyramids, globes, and poodles. We doubt that many Lazy Gardeners would have the temperament or interest for this kind of work, but there's no reason why you shouldn't become an efficient "creative" pruner in your own yard.

We use the word "creative" with great deliberation. Pruners in this world are divided into two classifications—hackers and the creative kind. A hacker merely chops at plants to get rid of unwanted growth. A creative pruner doesn't lay shears to wood until he's studied a plant and formed in his mind an exact picture of its redesigned structure.

Let's trace your thoughts and actions as you stand before some overgrown monster in your shrub border. You proceed cautiously through four steps.

Step #1: Cut out all dead wood. You need have no hesitation about this. Wade right in after the kindling with the appropriate cutting instrument. Even in midwinter, with a deciduous plant, you can easily distinguish a dead branch from a live one. When in doubt, bend a twig. If it snaps, it's firewood.

Step #2: Having cleaned the plant of dead encumbrances, examine it again carefully. The remaining branch structure is the marble you're going to sculp with and you don't want a slipped chisel. Use a negative approach. Cut off all twigs, crossed branches, and sucker growth you're clearly *not* going to want in your finished design. If in doubt, don't cut—yet.

Step #3: Now we come to the moment of truth, as they say in the bullfighting dodge. You're through with snipping and snapping. You've got to commit yourself to some major cuts and you'd better be right.

Study the shrub again, possibly with a drink in hand to steady your nerves. Examine each remaining branch, running your eye from ground level to topmost twig, then back again. (If it's an Evergreen shrub you might temporarily tie back obscuring branches.) Which cut will help you achieve the structure you want, which will ruin it?

Having made your decision, fix your eye on the exact spot of execution and advance boldly. Cut, and haul the severed branch out of the way. Then return to your point of vantage and look again.

"You'll find that the first major cut tends to clarify where the next must be made—and the next and next in logical sequence. It gets easier as you go along. Only that first cold plunge is icy.

Step ⅏4: All that remains is a little cleanup work—snipping off broken and protruding branches and putting to rout a couple of dead twigs which eluded you previously. And of course you'll squirt tree wound compound on any cuts thicker than a fat pencil. This phase of the work can be fun—the polishing of the marble after the statue stands revealed.

Having established a basic philosophy and attack on creative pruning, let's apply your expertise to a couple of specific examples. Since in each case we'll be contemplating major surgery, January or February would be the best time for deciduous shrubs, March for Broad-leaved Evergreens.

Let's assume you own a bushy plant at the edge of your property which might conceivably block out an ugly telephone pole and transformer across the street if it were only four feet higher.

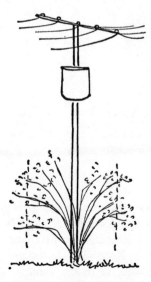

Original form of shrub

Problem: How to prune to force top growth?

Solution: Study the plant and note every upright-growing stem inside the bush. If you're dealing with an Evergreen, you can cut away leaves and side twigs to see better.

Begin pruning, cutting off all the obvious weeping and lateral growth first. Later cut (at ground level) major stems which are crooked or growing outward. Continue cutting until you've cleaned the bush of all but healthy upright stems. *Don't* prune anything off the top of these stems. They'll need every bud that's set.

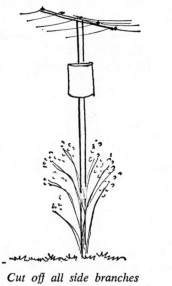 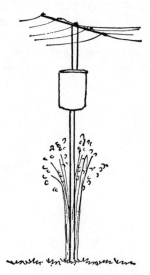

Cut off all side branches and crooked stems

Now only healthy, upright stems are left

When spring comes, the shrub's top growth should really take off, since all the plant's food and energy is directed to it. We don't promise the full four feet the first year, but it should do it in a couple of seasons. Keep side shoots cut off, though you can let root suckers grow to fill in the plant.

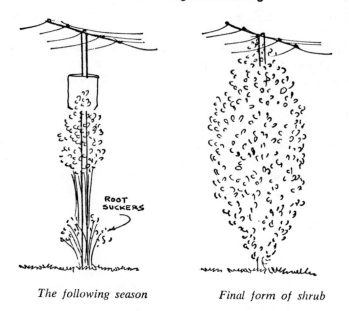

The following season   *Final form of shrub*

Let's take another example. We mentioned the possibility that you may have left a tall, gangling plant against the house because its leaves looked cheerful from your bedroom window. Good pruning practice would suggest turning it into a multi-trunked "Standard"—a nurseryman's name for a shrub trained as a small tree.

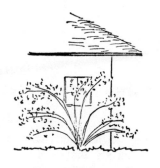

Shrub before pruning

Here's how it's done.

Again study the shrub. You're on firmer grounds this time since it's already at the height you want. Also since you're going to construct a tree, you know you don't want too many trunks—three at most.

You can cut out flopping and sideways-growing stems and branches immediately. Then, to help you visualize how your finished tree will look, "trunk up" the remaining stems—i.e., cut off all twigs and side branches up to "tree height."

Now you should be able to choose two or three main stems and remove the rest. Paint all cuts over half an inch with tree wound compound.

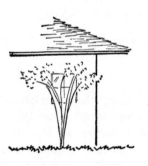

Cut off flopping stems and "trunk up" remainder.

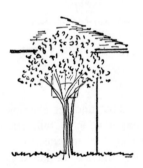

Final appearance (after growth matures)

PRUNING TECHNIQUES

Back in the chapter on tree pruning, we promised a full discussion on the hows, wheres, and whys of making pruning cuts. The technique is exactly the same for all woody plants. First let's start with the equipment you'll need.

PRUNING TOOLS

Anvil type   *Scissor type*

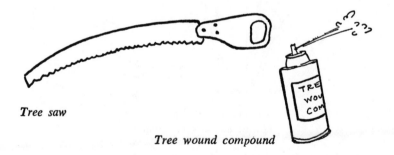

Long-handled pruning shears

Tree saw

Tree wound compound

Use your hand shears for cuts up to the thickness of a fat pencil. Switch to the long-handled loppers for thicker limbs but, no matter how new and sharp they may be, move to the tree saw for cuts of more than one inch in diameter. Excessively heavy cuts can strain scissored instruments. They lose their "set" and thus their ability to make clean, sharp incisions.

Where to Cut — and Why

Pruning experts instruct you to cut back to "the nearest lateral." This translates as: "Remove an entire unit of growth with each cut." You'll see what's meant in the following sketches.

Cutting a twig back to its nearest lateral

Cutting a branch back to its nearest lateral

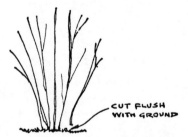

Cutting a stem back to its nearest lateral (the ground)

There are two reasons for pruning this way:
Aesthetic Reason: "Coat hangers" are ugly.
Biological Reason: "Coat hangers" encourage adventitious growth. What is adventitious growth?

A shrub or tree, if undisturbed, tends to set growth buds in more or less regular patterns along its branches. But if a branch is cut off, the plant responds by developing a group of emergency (adventitious) buds around the cut. These grow into a cluster of new shoots which are unsightly and tend to defeat your purpose in taking the branch off in the first place.

A sharp cut close to another branch reduces the number of adventitious buds which *can* be set. The following sketches show why.

"COAT HANGER" PRUNING

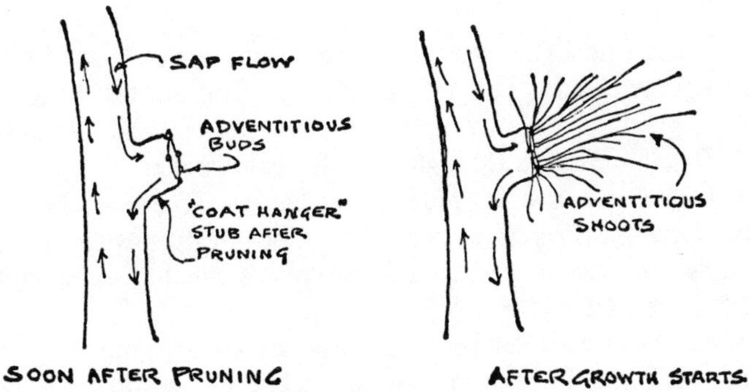

SOON AFTER PRUNING

AFTER GROWTH STARTS

Coat hanger pruning

CORRECT PRUNING

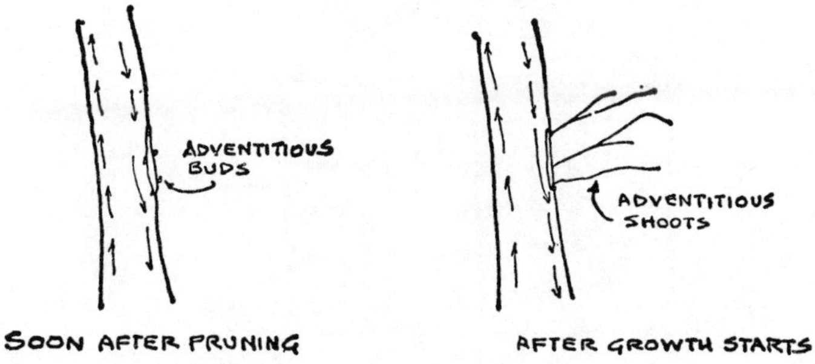

SOON AFTER PRUNING

AFTER GROWTH STARTS

Correct pruning

Some pruning authorities advise cutting at least a quarter of an inch from a lateral. But this seems pointless. A quarter-inch coat hanger is still a coat hanger. Also the old advice to make a slanting cut so that water will roll off seems unnecessary. Your tree wound compound should ward off any danger of rot.

So far we have been discussing techniques for creative "open" pruning. But there are a couple of "closed" techniques which we should consider—espaliering and hedge shearing. Each can prove useful to the Lazy Gardener.

Espaliering

Perhaps, when you were thinning shrubs around the foundation of your home, you left a sprawly plant in the hope that there might be some way of training it up a bare and windowless wall. It can be done through an informal espalier.

A *formal* espalier is quite a production. The idea was developed by the French to train fruit trees against walls and, by the time one was shaped to a Frenchman's satisfaction, a couple of lifetimes had passed.

When Americans adopted the idea we took it out of formal clothes and put it in shirt sleeves, and it has worked out very effectively for us too. The following sketches will illustrate the contrasts.

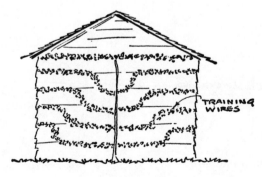

Formal espalier

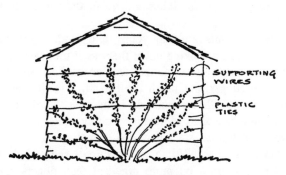

Informal espalier

To make an informal espalier, lift up your sprawling shrub and hold it against the wall to calculate how many transverse wires you'll need to support it. Drive in galvanized, rustproof nails and stretch galvanized wire between them. Lift and tie (with plastic ties) the main stems of your plant to the wires. Prune off the rest of the stems.

That's all there is to it. In effect, you're making a vine out of a shrub. Every couple of years you may want to climb up a ladder to add wires, or you can maintain the espalier at a predetermined height. Forsythia, Bridal Wreath, and Philadelphus all lend themselves well to this treatment.

Several shrubs are rigid and woody enough to scramble up walls without wires. Pyracantha is outstanding in this respect through most of the country. In warmer sections, Evergreen Pear and Lavender Starflower are often used. The espalier feeling is obtained by pruning. Branches which grow outward from the wall are cut back to their laterals. Branches which grow sideways or upward are encouraged.

If you buy a new shrub to start an espalier, plant it as close to the foundation as possible. Remember exposure. Explain to your Garden Center salesman the sun or shade conditions your wall offers. He'll help you select a lively plant which will flourish there.

Hedge Shearing

This is one form of pruning in which adventitious growth is wanted. In fact, it's the whole bit. The more new growth which springs from cut twigs, the fuller and richer the surface texture of your hedge.

When hedge plants are still young and tender, you can encourage bushiness by walking down them as if they were a chorus line, "pinching" as you go. Grasp any protruding twig between thumb and forefinger and pinch the tip off. Use the same technique for removing flower buds or fruits which may set on the shrubs. Pinching is a kind of manual pruning which directs all the plant's energies toward stem and leaf growth.

Once the hedge has filled in and matured, shears (electric or hand-held types) are a bit more practical than fingers. Clipping a hedge is something like driving a car; to maintain a straight line you must keep your eyes well down the road. Of course, the parallel can't be taken too literally. The sheer mechanics of cutting twigs requires more concentration than hanging on to a steering wheel. But as often as possible sight ahead fifteen or twenty feet to "keep your line." This will prevent the bellyings in and out which disfigure the look of a badly clipped hedge.

Trimming the top of a hedge, straight and flat, can be a problem. Unless you are very expert, a taut string stretched immediately below your cutting line can be an indispensable guide.

Correct hedge shearing

Sloppy hedge shearing
(*with leggy look*)

One more tip on hedge shearing: Keep the bottom wider than the top so that light can reach all sections. Otherwise the lower leaves and twigs will tend to die off, leaving your hedge with a "leggy" look.

Chapter 18

TRANSPLANTING—FERTILIZATION AND IRRIGATION

Possibly at the Garden Center you noticed that a certain kind of shrub was kept in full shade.* You own a similar shrub, but in your garden it's out in full sun and suffering because of it. When should you transplant?

Obviously as soon as possible, no matter what the season. You've nothing to lose but a sickly plant and you may eventually nurse it back to health by quick action.

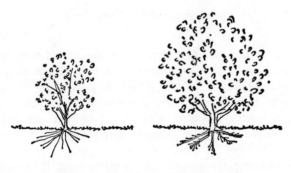

Fibrous roots   *Woody roots*

Shrubs up to a certain age and size—let's say three years old and three feet high—aren't too difficult to transplant since their roots are still more fibrous than woody.

---

* Garden authorities recognize two gradations in shade: Full shade (meaning shade all day) and partial shade, which is either half-day shade (preferably the second half) or dappled sunlight, as through the leaves of trees or under lath strips.

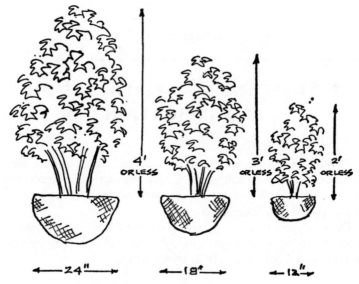

Approximate sizes of root balls

There's no hard and fast formula for the size of root ball you should attempt to lift (the sketches are only meant as guides), but obviously the more roots you take the better your chances for a successful transplant. Be careful not to shake off soil in transit from one hole to another, irrigate deeply and top prune as needed (severely if you've obtained few roots, otherwise a light trim).

If you contemplate transplanting a shrub taller than three feet and older than three years, better think of it as a tree. Wait till spring, if possible, and apply the principles described in Chapter 12 for tree transplanting.

New shrubs obtained from your Garden Center can be safely transplanted at any season they are offered for sale. You might consider working organic matter (see Chapter 24) into the soil you use to fill in around roots. Organic materials aerate the earth, make it more porous, and help water and fertilizers to penetrate. They're not absolutely necessary but can get shrub (and tree) transplants off to a faster start.

Never fertilize shrubs immediately after transplanting. Water, and water alone, is all that's required to start roots functioning. Fertilizers force demands which delicate tissues are unable to meet. To coin another horticultural ditty:

Till new roots grow—H_2O.
When new leaves flourish—nourish.

FERTILIZATION

You can fertilize shrubs strictly on a looks basis. If a plant looks healthy and has grown big enough for its location, don't sound the dinner gong. If you want more growth, serve the vittles.

Feed sun-loving shrubs with the fertilizer recommended for trees—blood meal. Scatter a handful around a small plant—two around a larger one—and soak the nutrients down to the roots with hose water. A couple of feedings—spring and early summer—should stimulate your shrubs into all the growth it's reasonable to expect in a season.

For shade-loving plants we recommend cottonseed meal. It too is organic, meaning that it's derived from a natural (as opposed to chemical) source. It's sold in a dry form, usually packaged in ten-pound bags. As with all organics, its nutrients are released slowly, becoming available to plant roots when temperatures and growing conditions are favorable. In addition, cottonseed meal tends to promote the acidity of soil.

We don't propose to discuss here the difference between "acid" and other soil reactions. The subject would hold as much interest for a Lazy Gardener as a debate on how many angels can dance on the head of a pin. It's enough to say that many shade-loving shrubs (among them, Azaleas, Camellias, Rhododendrons) prefer acid soils and cottonseed meal both fertilizers and acidifies. Apply a couple of handfuls per plant. Disperse the material around the "drip line" and water down to the roots. Two fertilizations, spring and summer, are enough for one season.

IRRIGATION

Shrubs generally are pretty rugged and, except for recent transplants, are not demanding about water. In areas of summer rainfall you'll rarely need to provide them with extra drink, though in times of drought and emergency lawn irrigation, it would be kindhearted to splash water their way. In dry summer climates, sprinkler systems normally take care of shrub needs.

Shade-loving shrubs tend to be more exacting in their moisture requirements than sun lovers. Some insist on constantly damp (not soggy wet) soil and sulk if this isn't provided. Camellias are notorious in this respect, especially at blossoming season. If moisture isn't precisely to their liking, they react by dropping buds. This can be checked by a two-inch mulch which prevents evaporation and also tends to absorb excess water.

Chapter 19

SHRUB PESTS AND DISEASES

You grow shrubs mainly for their shiny leaves and leaves attract pests. (Shrubs with scales instead of leaves, like junipers, attract fewer pests.) But the rule of health we've noted for your lawn grasses holds good for shrubs. Pests are quicker to attack sickly plants than vigorous growers, so your best protection against them is effective shrub maintenance.

Still, in spite of your best efforts, pests and diseases will invade.

PEST CONTROL

Spring is the time when insects are most active. Aphid are around then; so are mealybugs. White flies get tired of being eaten by trout and come over to eat in your garden. All these pests will go away eventually and, unless the invasion has been severe, won't leave irreparable damage behind. Still, it's unpleasant to have nameless things buzzing around and irritating to find your prized shrubs shot through with holes and teeth marks. Chances are you'll want to repel them when they appear. That means spraying with insecticides.

Spraying shrubs calls for a different type of dispenser than you've been using for your lawn. Lawn guns lay down too coarse a spray. A shrub dispenser atomizes chemicals into a fine mist. Often a "sticker" is added to the bottled solution to insure that the mist clings to the leaves, thus holding the poisons in place till an insect starts eating.

SHRUB SPRAY DISPENSER

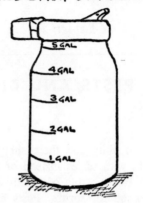

Shrub spray dispenser

You'll notice from the sketch that often the dispenser jar is only graduated up to five gallons as against the fifteen gallons of most lawn guns. This is because the misty spray is used up slowly and not as much is needed.

Ask your Garden Center salesman to recommend a general shrub and garden insecticide. If the directions on the bottle call for one tablespoon per gallon, drop in five tablespoons of the concentrate and fill the jar up to the neck with water. Then experiment in your garden to determine if this is enough to cover your shrubbery.

No formula tells you how much spray to use per shrub. Just apply the mist until the leaves and twigs are thoroughly covered, inside and out, above and below. Then move on to the next shrub. You can attach your dispenser jar to a pistol grip nozzle, as you did for lawn spraying, and save yourself steps if you have to refill.

How many times a year will you have to spray to keep your shrubs reasonably clear of bugs? It depends on invasions. With luck, you may not have to spray at all. In a bad year, two or more applications may be necessary. (*Note:* We're speaking here only for general ornamental shrubs, *not* Roses, which are a completely different story—see Chapter 20.)

DISEASE CONTROL

Fungal diseases sometimes attack shrubs in the form of mildews and blights. But they aren't a constant menace—except again for Roses. If diseases occur, they can be controlled by a sulfur based fungicide. Since you'll probably be spraying for pests at least once during a season, add a fungicide—usually packaged in powder form—when you load up your jar, just as a precautionary measure.

Lately, a copper-based fungicide has been developed which can be bottled with insecticide chemicals (as sulfur can't). We've tested the mixture and find it works well, both with general ornamentals and Roses. If your Garden Center stocks it, use it by all means. It'll save you steps in opening packages and mixing, worthwhile economies for any Lazy Gardener.

Flower Maintenance

To be brutally frank, a section on flowers should have no place in this book. To produce blossoms of any quality means unremitting toil, sweat, and tears. Because of the ultimate rewards, these conditions are accepted, even enjoyed, by certain undaunted and aspiring spirits. But that description hardly seems to fit the image of the work-resistant Lazy Gardener we've been holding before us.

Possibly you don't take us seriously. You've studied our recommendations for lawn, tree, and shrub care, and found the work involved not too taxing. What's so different about flowers?

Their physical structure is the difference. Trees and shrubs are woody plants. Their tough stems and leathery leaves offer few temptations to insects and fungal growths looking for a meal. But flowers (in the florist's sense) grow on herbaceous plants, soft-stemmed, with tender, succulent leaves. Pests find them as irresistible as chicken dinners with all the fixin's.

If you want a practical tip on an easy way to take care of flowers, grab a shovel and root out any you now possess. Stick with lawns, trees, and shrubs (and, by all means, ground covers, which we'll come to later) and you can remain a relaxed and lazy gardener with a song in your heart and time on your hands. Start in on flowers, and demons will arise to haunt you.

You won't heed our advice, of course. You have too many memories of the perfect flowers Mother used to grow, or Uncle Ned, or the lady up the street. You're impatient for us to stop our nonsense and get on with telling you how it's done.

Very well. Bunyan wrote *Pilgrim's Progress* to warn of the pitfalls which lurk for the unwary. Dante wrote *Purgatory* to etch in lurid detail the penalties for headstrong action. It's in the same spirit that we undertake our section on flower maintenance. If what we have to recount leaves you pale and shaken, we can only hope that you'll finally take us seriously while there is yet time.

We'll begin with the worst first—Roses.

Chapter 20

ROSES

Just to complicate things, Roses don't bloom from herbaceous stems as do Zinnias, Asters, and Snapdragons. They bud and blossom from woody branches. Technically, we should have placed them in the shrub section, not here. But imagine the screams if we had. In song and story, romance and legend, a Rose is a flower, and that's all there is to it.

In one form or another, Roses have been around a long time. They were known way back in history when the Medes were having trouble with the Persians. The Crusaders get credit for introducing them into Europe and they brightened up many a medieval monastery during the Dark Ages. They crossed to this country with the Pilgrim Fathers—cultivated varieties, that is—you could hardly step out with your squirrel gun without tripping over sturdy native Roses.

We know more about the ancestry of cultivated Roses than any other flower. For instance, the blooms which started the Wars of the Roses were single-petaled, not much advanced over wild species. Musk Roses came in about Shakespeare's time. Father Hugo's Rose, still a standard, was imported from China in the last century. Slowly, through cross-pollination and selective breeding, Roses were improved in size, fullness of flower and length of blooming season. But it wasn't until comparatively recent times, when the principles of hybridization became better understood, that the Rose was transformed into the spectacular, constant-blooming exhibition flower we know today.

Of course, with all this emphasis on blossom, something had to give and, not surprisingly, it was the constitution of the plant. The modern pedigreed Rose bush has almost totally lost its resistance to pests and diseases. Though a woody, deciduous shrub,

it's unable to survive winter frosts without protection. It's even
unable to fulfill its destiny of colorful and continued blossoming
without copious applications of fertilizer.

In short, consider the Roses in your garden as both master-
pieces of the hybridizer's art and aristocratic weaklings, incapable of functioning without spoon feeding.

WINTER PROTECTION

In the northern two-thirds of the nation, your spoon feeding
starts in autumn, right after the first frost. Pile a cone of earth
around the shrub's lower stems, hopefully eighteen inches high
but you can get away with a foot. When built, the earth cone
should be firmed with the back of your shovel or your foot.

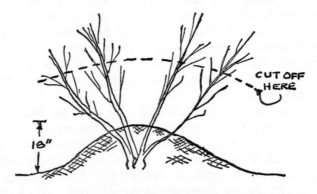

Earth cone mounded around rose stems

The purpose of the cone is to protect at least six inches of
your Rose canes. Otherwise they'll be dried out and killed by
winter winds. Consider the branches which extend beyond the
cone as already dead and cut them back by about half. The
mounded earth also protects your plant's roots from the alternate action of thaws and freezes, which might heave them from
the ground.

SPRING CARE

In spring, when night temperatures are consistently above forty degrees, remove the earth cone carefully. (Washing it off with a fine hose spray is sometimes recommended.) Examine the canes and prune off the dead ends, cutting back to green wood. Last step: Dig a watering basin around each Rose bush deep enough to expose the "bud union."

What is the bud union?

All registered Roses (the only kind worth spending time and money on) are grafted. Where rough rootstock and desirable Rose variety (the "named" Rose you bought) are joined together, a kind of callus develops which is called the bud union.

It's important to keep the bud union above ground during the growing season because shoots which develop around the callus grow into desirable Rose-bearing canes, while shoots from below are suckers and should be torn off. The elevated bud union allows you to see which is which.

WARM WINTER ROSES

If you live in a warm winter region, you can omit the frost protection for roots and canes. The fact is, you could probably keep cutting a few Roses right through St. Valentine's Day and into spring. But resist the temptation. By mid-February at latest, sharpen up your shears and start pruning. It takes courage to reduce a leafy bush to a few barren sticks, but you're doing it for the plant's own good. It's important for future flower production to denude the shrub of all leaves. This forces it into dormancy, if only for a brief period.

How many canes should you leave on a pruned shrub? From three to five, well distributed around the bud union. Height of canes? From two to three feet for Teas and Grandifloras, less for Floribundas.

SPRAYING AND FEEDING PROGRAM

Now—for all gardeners in all climates and regions—the fun really begins. When the first leaves appear, you start spraying against pests and diseases. You use your shrub dispenser which sprays with a fine mist. You load it with the same combination of pesticides* and fungicide as was recommended for your ornamental shrubs (Chapter 19). From spring until first frost you spray *every* week. To skip a week is to invite disaster.

Feed your Roses once a month using a fertilizer high in phosphorus. You'll remember from a previous discussion (Chapter 3) that phosphorus stimulates stem and root growth. It also promotes flower and seed production, and flowers are the prize

---

* High labor-saving hopes were aroused a few years ago with the introduction of the "systemic" pesticides. Poisons, drawn in by the roots and leaves, were supposed to permeate a plant's entire physiological structure (flowers included), thus spelling instant death to any nibbling insect. In our experience, systemics haven't proved that fatal. Besides, they make no provision for disease control, especially mildews. If you have to spray for anything, you may as well spray for everything and be safe.

you're after. A "complete" fertilizer analyzing about 4-12-4 should do the trick. We recommend applying it in a dry, granular form, often found packaged at your Garden Center under the label "Rose Food." Scatter the recommended amount over the root zone of your shrub and soak down with water. It's a great convenience to have a hose bib close to your Rose bed. Any week it doesn't rain, you'll have to irrigate by filling the basins. Roses are known as gross feeders, but they also swig more than is respectable.

PRUNING DURING GROWING SEASON

Remember that every time you cut blossoms for the house you are also pruning. Keep the center of the shrub open and clear of crossed branches, thus forcing buds to set on the outside where they can obtain better light and air and grow longer stems. Of course, you'll keep snipping off spent blossoms; otherwise part of the plant's strength will go toward the production of seed which is only useful to you if you're addicted to Rose hip tea.

Chapter 21

FLOWER CLASSIFICATIONS

As we have noted, flowers in the florist's sense (Roses ex-
cepted) grow from soft-stemmed, succulent herbaceous plants.
You recognize some (Daffodils, Phlox, Shasta Daisies) as permanent residents in your garden. Others (Petunias, Zinnias, California Poppies) are transients, livening up the summer but dis-
appearing with the autumn frosts.

Let's inquire into this differing behavior. You can best help
your flowers if you know what they're trying to achieve during
a growth cycle. You can also help yourself by learning how to
thwart some of their natural instincts for your own very human
purposes.

Let's begin by surveying three general classifications of herbaceous flowering plants—perennials, annuals, and biennials.

1. PERENNIALS

Perennial plants, as their name suggests, aim to be around,
if not forever, at least for a good few years. They are equipped
to weather hard winters and, though their tops die down, their
underground systems remain intact and primed to swing into
action with the coming of spring.

New growth develops on perennials from buds set on fibrous
roots or from the stored energy of bulbs, tubers, corms, and
rhizomes. Examples from each category are:

Perennials from fibrous roots	*Perennials from bulbs, tubers, corms, and rhizomes*
Astilbe	Anemone
Bleeding-heart	Crocus
Chrysanthemum	Daffodil
Columbine	Hyacinth
Coral-bells	Iris
Delphinium	Lily
Lupine	Peony
Phlox	Snowdrop
Shasta Daisy	Tulip

We have purposely left off our lists some spectacular flowering plants which form the heart of many perennial gardens. Examples are:

Amaryllis	Gladiolus
Dahlia	Tuberose

Our reason for omitting them is that they aren't true hardy perennials which will weather frosty winters. Their corms and tubers must be lifted and protected indoors to keep them from freezing, and that seems a bit much to expect of a Lazy Gardener.

Even in warm climates, where frost is not a problem, these plants must be dug after flowering or rot will set in.

Perennials are the mainstay of most flower gardens. They range in height from the six-foot blossoming spires of Delphiniums to the inch-high colored flecks of Snowdrops and Crocuses. Among the plants we've listed, something will be in bloom from early spring to late autumn. But there will be times when the color show will lag and you'll turn gratefully to flowers of another classification—annuals.

2. ANNUALS

Annuals are plants in a hurry. In a single season they must germinate from seed (some so tiny that you have to polish up your bifocals to see them), grow to full maturity (a Sunflower to nine feet), blossom, and set new seed before frost carries them away. This takes some doing and an annual doesn't have much time to fight poor conditions if it's going to be a success. It needs all the help it can get from you (good soil, right exposure, fertilizer, and water) to bloom profusely and continuously.

Some easy-to-grow, good performing annuals are:

Annuals under 12 inches	Annuals from 1 to 2 feet	Annuals higher than 2 feet
Ageratum	Balsam	Coreopsis
Forget-me-not	Calendula	Cosmos
Lobelia	California	Flowering
Mignonette	Poppy	Tobacco
Nasturtium	China Aster	Larkspur
Petunia	Cockscomb	Lavatera
Portulaca	Four-o'clock	Marigold
Sweet Alyssum	Madagascar	Spiderflower
Verbena	Periwinkle	Sunflower
	Snapdragon	Zinnia
	Stock	

Since you probably want bloom as early in the season as possible, it's a waste of time to try growing annuals from seed. Let the professionals start them off in their hothouses. You buy them from your Garden Center as small plants ("sets") and get a jump on the weather. With some plants which originated in tropical regions (Marigolds and Zinnias, for instance) there's no point in putting them into the ground before night temperatures reach forty-five degrees. They just won't grow and might possibly get nipped off by a late frost. Keep your eye on the Garden Center shelves. When sets are offered for sale it's because the time is right for your neighborhood.

Forget-me-nots may begin to bloom in May, but don't expect much flower action from other annuals until considerably later. Still, it all works out well. When the big flush of perennial blossoms (Tulips, Daffodils, Peonies, Delphiniums) dies down, the annual show will be just beginning. It will continue, along with the middle and late season perennials (Phlox, Lilies, Chrys-anthemums), until ice forms on the birdbath. Your hands will be callused by that time and you'll be a stranger to your family, but deep in your heart you'll have a picture-postcard glow as you survey your Hollyhocks and Canterbury Bells—both, incidentally, biennials.

3. BIENNIALS

You might call biennials lazy annuals. They take two years to accomplish what annuals do in one. The first season they germinate, push up some top growth, then quit. It isn't until the second year that they get on with the climactic work of manufacturing flowers, setting seed, and dying.

There might be some justification for this lackadaisical behavior with towering plants like Hollyhocks and Foxgloves. Year one sets solid foundations, you might think, while year two builds up the skyscrapers. However, this reasoning breaks down with midget plants like Pansies, which also take two seasons to complete their cycles. So until plant psychiatrists come up with a better explanation we'll just have to put biennials down as half-time laggards in the garden.

Their roll call is short. The following are the only ones you're likely to run across in an unadventurous horticultural career:

Canterbury Bells	Iceland Poppy
English Daisy	Pansy
Foxglove	Siberian Wallflower
Hollyhock	Sweet William
Honesty	

In actual practice, biennials are treated as annuals. You buy plants with the first year's growth already behind them, ready to get down to business now without any more lollygagging.

Chapter 22

PERENNIAL BEDS AND BORDERS

Let's assume you already own some perennials in your front yard. There's a Peony clump up against the house, some Irises under a tree, and assorted clusters of Shasta Daisies and Chrysanthemums hither and yon.

These plants bloom in their seasons but somehow the results are disappointing. The patches of color are too dispersed and inconsequential to generate much excitement. You wonder if there isn't a better way to display your flowers.

Your answer could be a perennial bed or border. (There's a distinction between the two as we shall see.) By concentrating your plants you'll multiply their floral effects. You'll also subtract from your work in weeding, feeding, and watering them.

The success of a perennial bed or border depends on three factors:

1. Location
2. Arrangement of plants as to height
3. Selection of plants for continuity of bloom.

Let's examine these factors separately.

1. LOCATION

Any location that gets full sun and free circulation of air is ideal for growing perennials. We sketch three possible locations for beds or borders, noting the distinction between the two types of planting.

Perennial beds at entrance walk. Access on all sides.

Perennial border along front property line. Some access through split rail fence, complete access from sidewalk.

You'll note that the planting areas are modest in size. In the first sketch the two beds on either side of the front walk should total no more than a hundred square feet. In the second sketch the perennial border is cut back only three or four feet from the sidewalk. In the third, the most ambitious project, the border is approximately twenty feet long and averages five feet in depth— enough to display a lot of flowers. The principle is to start small. If you get ambitious after a couple of seasons of floral success, you can easily extend the areas.

Perennial border along side property line. Access from lawn area only.

2. ARRANGEMENT OF PLANTS AS TO HEIGHT

In the last two illustrations the taller perennials should obviously be located at the rear of the bed (up against the split rail fence in one case and the hedge in the other). Work down in descending order of plant height to the outer edge of the bed. This will give a well-ordered appearance and allow each plant a full allotment of sun.

In the first picture we're dealing with beds (on either side of the walk) which have no defined backstop, so we must create a different arrangement of plants. Place the tallest in the center and work outward in descending order of height. The appearance of these freestanding beds can be improved if they are mounded up slightly, thus emphasizing differences in plant heights. Ornamental boulders can also be effective in giving focus.

For some estimate of plant heights, let's refer back to our list of perennials in Chapter 21. We're going to list them again strictly from a height standpoint.

Perennials Over 3 feet	Perennials 2 to 3 feet	Perennials 1 to 2 feet	Perennials under 12"
Delphinium	Astilbe	Bleeding-heart	Anemone
Lily	Chrysanthemum	Columbine	Crocus
Lupine	Iris	Coral-bells	Hyacinth
	Peony	Daffodil	Snowdrop
	Phlox	Shasta Daisy	
		Tulip	

Sometimes heights can be misleading. Take Coral-bells for instance. The flowers come out in tall slender whips and are gone by the end of July while the leaves, only a couple of inches above the ground, remain attractive all season. Therefore Coral-bells should be placed in front rows rather than middle ranks as their blossoming height seems to dictate.

You'll find out quirks of other flowers after a while and, if you exercise care, you needn't hesitate to transplant them forward or backward at almost any season. You'll also want to move your existing perennials into your newly formed beds. Early autumn is best for lifting established clumps; it gives the roots time to dig in before cold weather.

3. SELECTION OF PLANTS FOR CONTINUITY OF BLOOM

A well-planned perennial garden should be in continuous bloom from spring to frost. It's easy in May and June. Tulips, Daffodils, and Delphiniums are just a few bright stars in a galaxy of colors. But what do you do when the fireworks subside in early July? Phlox is helpful, so are some Daisies and Lilies, but otherwise the flower show is at a virtual standstill till Chrysanthemums come along after the equinox.

How do you fill the void? You fill it with annuals and biennials. Green Thumbers may howl at this ("Annuals in a *perennial* bed? I mean, really!"), but you won't be deterred by their narrow, puristic standards. You want color and you don't intend to waste your time haunting specialized perennial nurseries in order to get it. Not with a quicker and easier source close to hand.

You're going to bring home from your Garden Center containers of Sweet Alyssums and Portulacas to act as border plants. You'll use Petunias to cover the faded leaves of Tulips and Daffodils, which must be left on the plants till they die naturally since they are maturing food for next year's bulbs. Zinnias and Marigolds will help the Phlox carry the color burden at middle-eye level, while Hollyhocks will shoot up pink and white spires to peak the bed.

To get quick results, you'll want to purchase at least some annuals already in bloom. You should see a wide assortment of these at your Garden Center; so many and so tempting, in fact, that selection becomes difficult. A plant in a four-inch clay pot is a good practical size. Larger plants tend to wilt badly when transferred to your garden; smaller sizes are more efficiently bought in bulk lots. Sometimes well-developed annuals are sold in plastic containers known in the trade as "quarts," though "cups" would more accurately describe their actual size. A quart is about the equivalent of a four-inch pot.

Back home, wait for the sun to move off the beds in order to minimize wilt.* Then transplant, using a trowel to dig holes. The blade of a shovel, driven into the ground close by, provides a convenient ledge against which to knock out plants from pots. Slip the new plants into the ground, being careful not to break root balls, and firm the soil around them. Water immediately.

You can pinch back any plant which seems a bit floppy. It's a good idea to pinch off all blossoms, too, so that the plant can devote full energy to establishing its manufacturing system for the next couple of days. New buds and blooms will push out again within a week.

---

* Wilt, in a transplanting sense, is not to be confused with wilt in a disease sense. Transplant wilt means that the leaf demands for water are greater than the roots can provide immediately; hence a droopy look. It's a situation that will remedy itself overnight but can be minimized by transplanting in the cool of day, out of the hot sun. Disease wilt also results from water lack, but arises from organic plant damage and so is a much more serious condition.

With so much color flying around you may be concerned about clashes. You needn't be. It's a good bet that every flower in your garden has passed through the hands of hybridizers and these specialists are unusually sensitive to "difficult" colors. Discords, if they appear, can usually be traced to "volunteers"— seedlings of pedigreed plants which have reverted to aboriginal hues. These are often harsh magentas or grating violets, disturbing to the senses. Just pull out the offenders and harmony will be restored.

Chapter 23

FLOWERS FOR CUTTING

For many gardeners the main reason for growing flowers is to bring armloads into the house. Perennial beds and borders aren't much help in serving this purpose because they have their own color shows to maintain. Occasionally you may be able to snip off a few fresh Daisies or even smuggle in a dozen Chrysanthemums, but it's a sparse harvest for an indooors flower lover.

If you must have flowers in bulk you'd better plan on a separate cutting garden. You'll grow mostly annuals since they provide a longer season of sturdy, arrangeable blossoms. Since production is your primary goal and aesthetics secondary, we suggest that the logical location for your cutting garden would be your back yard.

Pick out the area carefully, choosing it for maximum air circulation and exposure to the sun. The site could be bang in the middle of the yard or tucked into a corner, depending on the solar path and the shade cast by trees and buildings. A minimum of six full hours of sunshine is necessary for satisfactory flower development.

Next let's give a thought to design—the physical arrangement of your garden for easy cultivation. Don't be too startled at the illustration which follows. It may look like a busted Ferris wheel, but actually it represents a reasonably efficient layout for growing enough annuals to stock a florist's shop.

The one permanent feature of this cutting garden is the galvanized iron pipe driven into the center of the design and protruding approximately two feet above ground. This is the focal point from which the location of the circular planting rows can be marked, scratched out by a stick tied to the end of a taut string. The pipe will remain year after year. You might fit it with a revolving seat, from which you can survey your plants while they are still small. Later, the seat could be replaced by a decorative scarecrow.

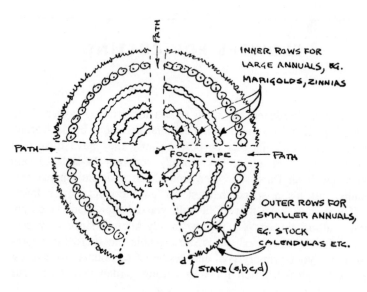

The "Flower Wheel" cutting garden

It's important to leave paths radiating out from the center for easy access to all areas. Also leave unplanted the pie-shaped segment indicated at the bottom of the drawing. You'll find it invaluable for maneuvering a hose in and out of the center island. Stakes driven in at points A, B, C, and D will protect plants from the hose's coils.

You'll locate your larger plants—Marigolds, Zinnias—around the inner circles, where they can obtain full height without shading outer rows. Scale down in sizes as you move toward the perimeter—Coreopsis, Stock, Snapdragons, and Calendulas. Save Daisies, Cockscombs, Cornflowers, annual Gaillardias, and perhaps Nasturtiums for the final circle, where they'll provide perky accents at the edge of what should be, in late summer, a mound of color.

Of course, you don't have to stick exclusively to annuals. You can divide Delphiniums from your perennial beds and find a place for them. Or accept gifts from your neighbor's division of his plants. You've only one criterion—is it truly a cutting flower, long-stemmed, long-lasting? Anything else can be clutter.

Spacing between rows will naturally depend on the area at your disposal, but try for at least two feet between rows of low flowers and three feet between taller ones. You're going to spend a good deal of time working down those circular alleys, and you don't want the feeling of breaking off branches every time you turn around.

Chapter 24

FLOWER BED PREPARATION

So far we've been generally successful in avoiding that dreadful topic—digging. But the time has come. Twist and turn as we may, there's no getting past the fact that worthwhile flowers can only be grown in thoroughly prepared soil. That means soil which has been tilled and pulverized to a depth of about eight inches (the depth of your shovel) and permeated with organic matter.

What is organic matter?

Peat moss is organic matter, so are sawdust, buckwheat hulls, coffee grounds, and just plain smelly farm manure. For centuries, well-rotted farm "dressing" was *the* staple organic substance, but in recent years gardeners have tended to shy away from it, not because of odor, but because of the weed seed it contains in its raw state.*

Organic matter conditions the earth. In heavy soils, it separates particles of clay, thus permitting freer penetration of water and fertilizers. In sandy soils, it creates texture, thus holding water which would otherwise sink away. It helps provide a growing medium where roots can perform at their maximum capacity—which means more and better flowers.

Perhaps the best form in which to buy organic matter is packaged, "nitrolized" sawdust. It's probably also the cheapest form available at your Garden Center. Just make sure of the words "nitrolized" or "with nitrogen added." Raw sawdust, for reasons we needn't go into here, tends to deplete the soil of nitrogen during the early stages of its decomposition and should be avoided.

---

* Manufacturers have countered by baking and sacking manure, which takes care of the seed (and much of the smell) but also robs it of organic value.

Now, if you're ready, let's proceed to the diggings. There are differences in preparing perennial beds and annual cutting gardens, so let's examine the technique for each separately.

SOIL PREPARATION FOR PERENNIAL BEDS AND BORDERS

Referring back to our sketches in Chapter 22, let's assume you're going to construct the perennial beds located on either side of the walk, though the principles are the same for any bed or border we've illustrated or you may devise.

There are five main steps.

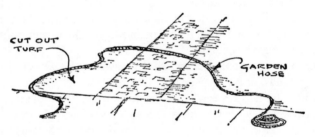

Step #1

Using your garden hose, outline a pleasing series of curves across lawns and front walk. Using your shovel, cut inside this line and remove sod to a depth of two inches. (Maybe you can use this turf to patch or extend your lawn elsewhere.)

Step #2

Spread nitrolized sawdust (or other organic matter) over the newly bared earth to a depth of two inches.

Step #3

Turn, churn, and till the organic matter into the ground, mixing it thoroughly with the soil. Keep doing this till the mixture is loose and friable to the full depth of your shovel.

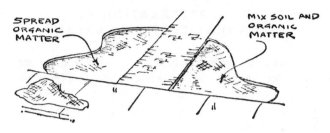

Steps #2 and #3

Step #4

Rake the area, further mixing materials and pulverizing clods. Remove sticks, stones, and other debris.

Step #5

Make mounds in the center of each bed by pulling soil up from the perimeter, leaving a two-inch furrow at the edge of lawn and pavements. Firm each mound by tapping it with the back of your shovel.

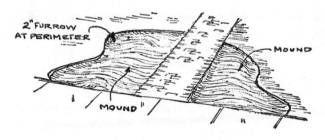

Steps #4 and #5

Your beds are now ready for planting. The surrounding furrows should catch excess rain or sprinkler water and keep lawn and pavements clean until plants cover the mounds. If it's spring or early summer, you can set out annuals immediately. But better wait till autumn before you plant perennials.

SOIL PREPARATION FOR
ANNUAL CUTTING GARDEN

Since you'll be dealing with a comparatively large area, time the work for comfortable weather conditions. This could mean spring, or autumn after the heat subsides. It *never* means midsummer, when your exertions could prepare *you* for the soil.

This time there are six steps.

Step #1

Tie a loop in a string and slip it over your focal galvanized iron pipe. Run the string out to the maximum radius of your design and, with a sharp stick or pointed spike, scratch out a circle. Using your shovel, clean out and pitch away all grass, weeds, or other matter which may be inside this circle. Reduce level of area by approximately two inches.

Step #2

Spread two inches of nitrolized sawdust or other organic matter over the cleared-off circle.

Step #3

Incorporate this organic matter into the earth by tilling, churning, mixing, to the full depth of your shovel. Continue till soil is loose and friable.

Step #4

Rake out and remove debris, constantly pulverizing soil to obtain finer texture.

Step #5

Hitch up your string again and mark out your circular planting rows in the soft earth. The sketch suggests how the area might look to a passing crow when you've finished. Don't forget to delineate the access paths.

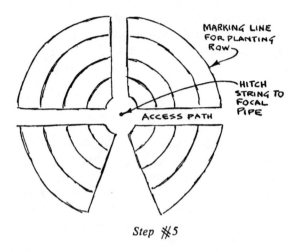

Step #5

Step #6

Using your shovel, move around the marked lines and pile them into circular, running mounds. The soil for mounding will come from either side of the lines. You should wind up with a sequence of curving hills, each about six inches high, with depressed walkways between them—broken only where the access paths cross.

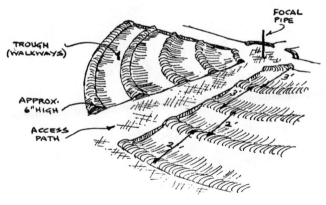

Step #6

Your cutting garden is now ready for planting. Of course, you'll plant on top of the mounds, not down in the troughs. If you've done your work well, you've put leisure time in the bank for the days ahead—as you'll see when we take up maintenance problems.

YOUR GARDEN HOSE

It's high time we said a word about your garden hose which has hardly been out of your hand since the beginning of this book. By all odds, it's your most important single piece of equipment, and you'll be doing yourself a favor by buying a good one.

Reinforced rubber (as against plastic) is the most satisfactory material. It's strong, light, long-wearing, and flexible—a quality you'll appreciate when you use your hose to lay out curves for garden beds. It comes in twenty-five and fifty feet lengths. Longer runs can be pieced together from these units. An inside gauge of 5⁄8 inch is recommended.

Chapter 25

FERTILIZING AND IRRIGATION

In a previous discussion (on feeding Roses) we made the point that phosphorus promotes flower and seed production. So phosphorus should obviously be prominent in the fertilizing formula used for both your perennial and annual gardens.

A "complete" fertilizer which analyzes 4-8-4 seems about right. The 4% nitrogen should encourage enough top growth to keep your plants a healthy green, without skyrocketing them at the expense of flowers. The 8% phosphorus is the key ingredient, aimed at producing sturdy stems and ambitious blossoms. While the 4% potash should insure steady root activity.

You can buy and apply your 4-8-4* fertilizer in liquid form, using your shrub gun to dispense it. Plants—all plants—can take in a certain amount of food through their leaves, so both the misty spray adhering to the foliage and the excess, dripping to the roots, stimulate growth. Because of this double action, you will naturally refrain from "washing down" your plants after a liquid feeding. You can rejoice, as you wind up your hose, at having saved yourself at least one chore so necessary in lawn fertilization (necessary because of the much higher concentration of nitrogen which can burn leaves). But just as a precaution, never spray-feed your flowers in the heat of day. Nitrogen, in whatever strength, is still nitrogen. Wait till the sun recedes and you can hear the cheerful tinkle of ice as cocktails are prepared.

Of course, you'll never in your right mind think of applying

---

* This formula is, of course, only approximate. Higher nitrogen percentages are permissible if in slow release, organic form. Also potash can vary up or down. Just make sure that the phosphorus ingredient, the performance factor, is adequate.

fertilizers (liquid or otherwise) to tender, newly transplanted flowers. A wilt can become a wake in jig time if you do.

How often do you fertilize?

Technically, a perennial only needs feeding twice: once before blooming (for this year's flowers) and once after blooming (for next year's). But since you spray a whole bed, not individual plants, and since perennials bloom at different seasons, it's difficult to control who's getting what, how often, and how much.

To complicate matters further, there are the annuals you've introduced into your perennial beds as temporary boarders. Do they need more or less food than the permanent tenants? And what about the annuals in your cutting garden?

What it boils down to is that you're like the old woman who lived in a shoe. You've too many children to give them individual attention. You'll just have to adopt an arbitrary feeding program around which the children must fit their meals as best they can.

We suggest a monthly schedule. Beginning on May 1, and as regularly thereafter as you pay your bills (or would like to), spray on a first-of-the-month basis until frost. Until June, you'll be concentrating mostly on your perennial beds, but by July your cutting garden will be beginning its big push and clamoring for food.

Just as important as fertilizer in producing prime blossoms is keeping spent flowers cut. Remember, you're playing an endless game with your plants—especially your annuals. For them, flower production is only a way station toward their ultimate goal —seed production. For you, flowers *are* the ultimate goal. So the more you keep cutting off blossoms, the more you force your plants to bloom again and again in their race against the season. Your home may be bulging with bouquets at the moment, but it won't be, a month from now, if you let your plants win the game and set seed on blossom pods you haven't bothered to cut.

IRRIGATION

It's so obvious as to be a bore that plants, to maintain health, must have moisture at root depth. But with herbaceous perennials it's not simple-minded to inquire—at what depth is that? Peony roots can take up residence two feet below ground level, while a Crocus housekeeps within the top two inches. When both are in the same bed, how do you irrigate one without flooding the other?

Annual roots are less dramatic in their depth variations, but their water requirements are equally exacting.

Let's look at irrigation techniques for both perennials and annuals in some detail.

Irrigating Perennials

In regions of winter snow and spring rains, you start the season with saturated soil—a full tank, as it were. The trick, later on, is to replace moisture as it evaporates or is used up by plant needs. As long as rains continue, you can whistle Dixie. But when dry weather comes, start checking.

In theory, keeping the top two inches of soil damp should compensate for normal moisture loss. But if, on a hot day, one of your deep-rooted perennials suddenly shows signs of wilt, forget about theory and run for your hose. Trickle water down beside your plant, and keep trickling until the leaves look flush again.

In regions of warm winters and summer drought, you won't have to worry about deep-rooted perennials like Peonies because they won't grow for you (see Chapter 27). But you have enough other problems—chiefly the matter of water distribution.

In a well-engineered sprinkler system, shrub heads and lawn heads are controlled by separate valves. But you may not be so fortunate with your sprinklers which, when turned on, provide a glorious but indiscriminate bath for everything within reach. Since perennials don't require—or welcome—as much water as your lawn grasses, this can create a dilemma.

Deep-watering your lawn not more than once a week (as recommended in Chapter 4) can help. But you may also have to cap off or screw down some sprinkler heads to prevent your flower beds from being flooded. If you construct new beds, mound them extra high to insure fast drainage.

Irrigating Annuals

If you've adopted our suggested design (Chapter 23) for an annual cutting garden—the Flower Wheel—irrigation during dry spells becomes child's play.

Build up dikes on either side of the access paths, then fill the troughs between the circular planting mounds with hose water. Let the water level rise till it's just on the verge of trickling over the mounds, then move the hose to the next trough. Moisture will permeate sideways and downward, thoroughly soaking the roots.

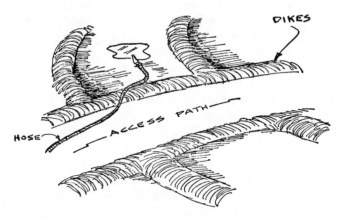

Irrigation with dikes

How often do you flood water in this way? It depends on your region and rains, of course. But, in any climate, you can test the condition of the soil by cutting into the sides of the mounds. If the soil is dry for half an inch, irrigate.

After you've become sure of yourself, you can also rely on visual tests. A well-watered plant has an unmistakable flush or "burgeoning" look. The look evaporates quickly when water runs out. If you keep a sharp watch, you can suspend irrigation until telltale signs of wilt, usually first visible on a hot afternoon. At which time you run—walking is too slow—for your hose.

In both perennial and annual gardens, make sure the ground is damp before the monthly feedings. Moist soil absorbs liquid fertilizer. Dry soil tends to repel it.

Chapter 26

PESTS, DISEASES, AND WEED CONTROL

There are some perennials—mostly of the bulb, tuber, corm, and rhizome fraternity—which are relatively immune to pests and diseases. Among annuals, Marigolds and Petunias are rarely seen crawling with wildlife or blotched by fungus. But the honor roll stops about there. Most other members of the herbaceous clan seem to attract undesirables like a free lunch counter on Skid Row.

Brace yourself for it—preventive measures must be taken.

There's no point in repeating all the sordid details of what must be done. It's all been covered before in connection with your shrubs and Roses (Chapters 19 and 20). Get out your spray dispenser. Pour in the same insecticides and fungicide (combined in a single mixture if you can find it—see Chapter 19—and let fly.

It's the same old story as with Roses. Hybridizers have bred resistance out of herbaceous plants too. They have little in common any longer with their rugged roadside relatives, who sneer at blights and mildews and, in some cases, actually eat pests. Garden flowers seem as helpless against the bludgeonings of chance as patients in a hospital ward.

Still, they're not *quite* as bad as Roses. You have to spray Roses *every* week, while you might get away with spraying your perennials and annuals every *other* week.

Take what comfort you can from that.

WEED CONTROL

Some people, if they're honest about it, get a therapeutic kick out of weeding. Upending a dandelion, dragging to light every last hair of its ugly root, seems to have a hidden significance— like exposing the Boss or showing up Mother. But for most of us, weeding is anathema. How can we escape the undignified crouch, the aching thighs and backs, the scuffed hands?

We can't, completely. They're the penalties of flower culture. But there are certain efficiency devices we can try, some adapted to perennial beds, others to the annual cutting garden.

Weed Control in Perennial beds

Empty spaces invite weeds—therefore plant closely. This is easy enough after the annuals come along, but what can you do in spring when your perennial clumps are showing bare ground between them?

You can apply a mulch.

What is a mulch?

A mulch is a blanket of organic matter (see Chapter 24) spread on top of the soil.* It performs several functions. Of immediate interest, it tends to stifle the germination of weed seed under it. It also helps prevent moisture evaporation and, as it decomposes, contributes to the texture of the earth.

Nitrolized sawdust makes an excellent mulch; so do buckwheat hulls, ground walnut and peanut shells with nitrogen added. Needless to say, your mulching material should itself be free of weed seed. It should also be interesting to look at, in either texture or color, to help "dress" your beds.

Peat moss, though it has many good uses, is not recommended for mulching. Reason: Though it absorbs water readily when

---

* Under Lawn Maintenance (in Chapter 2) we warned against mulches which "can cause rotting mats" because they are conducive to Ground Fungus. The situation here is entirely different. No matter how closely you plant herbaceous shrubs, you won't vaguely approximate the crowded condition of lawn grasses. Air will still circulate to relieve the menace of Ground Fungus.

damp, it repels moisture if it ever dries out—in which case irrigating through peat moss becomes almost impossible.

How thickly should a mulch be applied?

Start with an inch-deep blanket. As ground becomes exposed
again through wind and water action, add more material. If your
plants are well established, an initial two-inch blanket is not
excessive and will save the work of distributing more later.

Weeding tool

Despite close planting and mulching, however, weeds will
come—the toughest, most control-resistant ruffians of your garden. We've found that a particular hand tool, shaped like a flat-
tened claw hammer (as sketched), is most effective in uprooting
them.

Weed Control in the Annual Cutting Garden

If you've followed the Flower Wheel design suggested in
Chapter 23, you'll find you can weed, farmer style, with a hoe.
Just work around the rows, scuffing as you go. Most weeds are
annuals, so cutting them off just below the crown disposes of
them. You'll learn to recognize and root out the perennials because of their reappearance.

After cleaning out weeds, you may be able to apply a pre-
emergent herbicide, dusting it on the ground in powdered form
and soaking it in afterwards. Better consult with your Garden
Center salesman about this. Not all pre-emergents are recommended for use around flowers. Some can inhibit growth in
herbaceous plants.

Instead of using chemicals, you can mulch your annuals as a
weed control measure. You'll have to use a coarser material

than for your perennial beds, otherwise the mulch will float away when you flood water. Salt hay is ideal—if you live in an area where it's obtainable. Its seed won't germinate in your garden—only on tidal flats—so you don't import trouble when you use it—as you can with ordinary straw, no matter how well threshed. You can water right through the salt hay and, though some will float, it'll settle down again evenly.

Chapter 27

THE FLOWERS OF WARM WINTER CLIMATES

If you live in a snowbound winter region, you probably feel galloping envy when you see on television Rose parades and other evidences of blossoms in January. It's too much. The lucky stiffs can grow everything you can, and on a twelve-month basis.

Not so. Many spectacular flowers, common in your district, can't be grown in warm winter climates. They *require* frost to enable them to bloom from year to year. Of the eighteen herbaceous perennials listed in Chapter 21, only four (Chrysanthemums, Coral-bells, Shasta Daisies, and Irises) run true to type in Southern California. Others, such as Delphiniums, are grown as annuals and junked after blooming. Peonies and Astilbes can't be grown at all.

Of course there are perennial exotics never seen elsewhere except in florists' windows—Clivias, Birds-of-Paradise, Lilies of the Nile. But it's in the production of annuals that warm winter climates come into their own. Calendulas, Stocks, Snapdragons, Petunias, Marigolds, and Zinnias follow each other around the seasons in endless succession. The problem often is when to pull one crop and start another. It takes a ruthless hand to dispose of Snaps in their prime just because hot weather's coming and it's time to switch.

But don't get the erroneous idea that all is joy in winter sunshine land. It isn't. Take the matter of pests. Frost wipes out pests abruptly in most parts of the country. True, they've laid eggs and another generation will be along in the spring, but meanwhile there's surcease.

It's different in warm winter areas. Pests linger into ripe old age, piling generation on generation. Those flowers in the Rose parades have been sprayed so often they're 90 proof in chemicals. Even so, the girls riding the floats have a hard time. You think they're waving at you but, in reality, they're swatting at white flies.

Look at it this way: The Lazy Gardener in snowbound regions is the lucky stiff. He can rest for six months a year. It's his counterpart in the sunny South who's to be pitied. He has to be at it all the time.

Ground Cover Maintenance

In a sense, we've been talking about ground covers since the beginning of this book. Lawns are ground covers. Trees can envelop a landscape. Massed shrubs are certainly ground covers and, in perennial beds, the name of the game is to plant tight and hide the ground from everybody.

But ground covers—in a technical, garden sense—are something else. The name is most often applied to low-growing herbaceous plants which spread in neat mats across the ground, like Moss Pink or Basket-of-gold. As we'll see, there are other types and kinds of ground covers, but let's concentrate for the moment on the creeping perennials. They're colorful and vigorous and—best of all from the Lazy Gardener's point of view—low in maintenance requirements.

Why? Because the hybridizers have, by and large, kept their hands off them. Their flowers, depending on mass bloom for effect, were considered too insignificant for "improvement." So the plants remain almost as rugged as they were in their native habitats. Once established, they can hold their own against drought, pests, and diseases, and work better than chemicals at suppressing weeds.

But ground covers have more going for them than iron constitutions. Because of compact growth and rich texture, they possess design values too often overlooked. In decorator's terms, they're "unifiers"—like a new carpet which can suddenly pull together diverse elements in a room. In your garden, ground covers can unify scattered patterns of trees, lawns, and shrubs.

We'll delve into these and other matters later on. Meanwhile it's enough to observe that many Lazy Gardeners are of the opinion that a certain poet was barking up the wrong plant when he composed a tribute to a tree. He'd have been closer to the mark if he'd written:

> Poems are made by fools like me
> But only God can make I.V.

Chapter 28

GROUND COVER CLASSIFICATIONS

Though garden literature has done scant justice to ground covers, they were well known to celebrated authors of the past. Shakespeare, for instance, was plugging a creeping, herbaceous type when he describes "a bank where the wild Thyme blows." William Wordsworth advocated a less orthodox but still valid ground cover in his "host of golden Daffodils." Tennyson's brook burbled through a shade-oriented planting of ferns. While Moses, at one point in his career, was almost totally hidden by another ground cover—perhaps a trifle high for general garden use—bulrushes.

Ground covers don't stop with plants, either. Quite a few inanimate materials are included in the definition. The Scottish lass who called the cattle home across the sands of Dee was vocalizing over a well-known Oriental ground cover—sand. While the Biblical character, poised to cast the first stone, evidently had in mind laying down another—pebbles.

Moving on to specifics, we can arrange ground covers into three general classifications:

1. Perennial herbaceous ground covers
2. Shrub ground covers
3. Inert ground covers

1. PERENNIAL HERBACEOUS GROUND COVERS

As we have seen, this is the classic group. All on the following list are low-growing, or comparatively so. Some are creepers or trailers. Others are upright shrubs which should be closely planted for mass effects. Those which blossom only seasonally, then subside into neat foliage, are so marked: (Seas.). Continuous bloomers, once flowers appear, are also indicated: (Cont.).

You may be surprised to find us calling some plants "ground covers" which you see listed in nursery catalogues as "Rock Garden Specialties." That terminology is a holdover from the rockery craze which swept the country early in this century. While it lasted, no garden with any pretensions was without its pile of rubble. The moldering heaps have gone now, but we honor their memory for the many useful ground covers they introduced to cultivation.

Name	Exposure	Description
Ajuga (Bugleweed)	Shade or partial shade	Flat green (sometimes bronze) leaves, low, creeping —blue flowers in spring. 3″ high. (Seas.)
Basket-of-gold	Sun	Grayish leaves, bright yellow flowers in spring. 15″ high. (Seas.)
Bearberry	Sun or partial shade	Rich green foliage on reddish stems, creeper. Red berries in autumn. 6″ high. (Cont.)
Cotton Lavender (Santolina)	Sun	Grown for silver-gray foliage, flowers not important. 12″ high.
Creeping Thyme	Sun	Gray-green foliage, tiny leaves, spreads in low mats. Blue flowers in summer. 3″ high. (Seas.)
English Ivy	Shade or partial shade	Heavily veined, lobed leaves. Lies flat or climbs. Can pile up to 10″ high. No flowers.
Moss Pink	Sun	Green moss-like foliage. Especially neat mounds. Pink flowers in spring. 6″ high. (Seas.)

Name	Exposure	Description
Myrtle (Vinca, Periwinkle)	Shade or partial shade	Dark green leaves, trailing growth. Flowers May and June. 8″ high. (Seas.)
Pachysandra (Japanese Spurge)	Shade	Thick, dark, glossy leaves on stems 8″ high. Spreads by underground runners. No flowers.
Sedum	Sun	Many varieties, some quick-forming low mats, others tall (12″) and sedate. June bloom. Colors yellow, red. (Seas.)
Snow-in-Summer	Sun	Silver foliage, fast grower—white flowers begin in June. 8″ high. (Cont.)
Yellow Cinquefoil	Sun	Bright green strawberry-like leaves. Yellow blooms from June to frost. 3″ high. (Cont.)

Add for warm winter climates:

Name	Exposure	Description
Blue Fescue (Festuca)	Sun	Ornamental blue grass with neat tufts. 6″ high. No flowers.
Gazania	Sun	Both bush (green leaves) and trailing (gray leaves) types. Daisy-like flowers throughout year—yellow, gold, bronze. 6″ high. (Cont.)
Iceplant	Sun	Both bush and trailing types. Succulent. Fast grower. Spring flowers—all colors. 6″ to 12″ high. (Seas.)

Name	Exposure	Description
Ivy Geranium	Sun	Trailing geranium, ivy-like green leaves. Blooms most of year—red, pink, white. 8″ high. (Cont.)
Parrot's Beak	Sun	Feathery gray foliage, beak-like red flowers in summer. 6″ high. (Seas.)
Wild Strawberry	Sun	Dark green strawberry leaves. Scattered 1″ white flowers in spring. Fast grower. 6″ high. (Seas.)

Consider the plants in the foregoing list merely as "starter" suggestions. There are many more grown in your neighborhood. Ask your Garden Center salesman about them. He'll either have samples on hand or direct you to where they may be seen. He'll also be able to scan down our list and inform you which plants grow best in your district.

2. SHRUB GROUND COVERS

We noted in our section on shrubs that they can substitute for small trees, vines, and fences. They also perform important duty as ground covers. In fact, there are times when no other plants are as suitable.

Shrubs, since they are larger and more structured than herbaceous perennials, convey a greater feeling of substance and permanency. That's why you'll find them used so often outside of public buildings. Nobody wants a flighty atmosphere around City Hall.

Shrub ground covers also suggest formality. Again you will note their use around banks and expensive homes. It's unlikely that anyone consciously asks himself, "Am I a conservative shrub man or a gay-blade herbaceous type?" but often the appropriate plant material shows up outside his house.

Effective ground cover shrubs grow wide rather than tall. Some develop sideways, often with a recumbent habit; others arch, the tips of their branches touching the ground. All should present naturally neat and tidy patterns.

In the following list, evergreen shrubs are marked (E); deciduous shrubs (D). The first four are usually considered "hardy" (meaning they're proof against all but the severest winters), though you can only be sure about this in your section if they're offered for sale at your Garden Center.

Name	Exposure	Description
Compact Arborvitae	Sun	Dense low-grower. 2 to 4 ft. high. (E)
Creeping Yew	Sun or shade	Wide-spreading branches. To 3 ft. high. (E)
Prostrate Juniper	Sun	Graceful green side-thrusting branches. Scale-like leaves. 2 ft. high. (E)
Rock Spray Cotoneaster (pronounced: Ko-tone-ee-aster)	Sun	Arching habit. Small leaves. Red berries in winter. 1 to 2 ft. high. (D)

Add for warm winter climates (not hardy):

Name	Exposure	Description
Asparagus Fern	Sun or shade	Fern-like leaves on arching stems. 18″ high. (E)
Carmel Creeper	Sun	Glossy leaf, rapid growth. Blue flowers in spring. To 4 ft. high. (E)
Edward Goucher Abelia	Sun	Graceful arching habit. Lavender-pink flowers. To 4 ft. high. (E)
Prostrate Mirror Plant	Sun	Glossy leaves which reflect sun. 2 ft. high. (E)
Prostrate Natal Plum	Sun or partial sun	Brilliant green leaf. Large white flower followed by edible plum. 3 ft. high. (E)

Shrubs, of course, grow more slowly than herbaceous ground covers. Prostrate Junipers, planted three feet apart, will take approximately three years to meet. Meanwhile there is open ground between and, where there is open ground, there are weeds.

What to do?

Some people plant Sweet Alyssum seeds. Sweet Alyssum is an annual which grows at a rate to rival weeds. If the weather is right, they can develop from seed to first blossoms in six weeks. A couple of weeks later you'll have a billowy foam of flowers, three inches high, white or purple—you even get a choice of colors. Since the plants are annuals, they die off at the end of the season, but the seeds winter over and come back strong the following spring. With very little effort (occasional help in reseeding, perhaps) you can keep a carpet of Alyssum going year after year until one of two things happens: you get sick of Alyssum, or the permanent shrubs meet and shade them out. Usually the two things happen at about the same time.

Another approach to vacant spaces between growing shrubs is the use of inert ground covers.

3. INERT GROUND COVERS

Any inanimate material which lies flat and suppresses weeds could, in the widest sense, be called an inert ground cover. This would include concrete, asphalt, and flat-laid bricks. But in a garden sense, the term is usually applied to loose, workable, interestingly colored or textured materials, such as sand, gravel, granulated brick dust, shredded tree bark, or river-washed pebbles.

Sand: The Japanese perform miracles with sand in their gardens, piling it into miniature Mount Fujis, raking it into symbolic representations of rivers and oceans; but then they have a long time between cups of sake. For the Lazy Gardener there's too much work in keeping it clean and fluffing it up after rain has knocked it flat. A sandbox for the kiddies is enough of this particular substance.

Gravel: Gravel is practical for utility areas, such as clothes drying yards and garden paths, but it requires a certain amount of upkeep (mostly raking) to keep it looking like anything. Never use it under wheeled traffic. Even a bicycle can scatter enough segments to ruin your lawn mower. Natural pea gravel is dressiest, but crushed rock (¾ inch is a workable size) presents a good appearance and is less expensive.

Granulated Brick Dust: If you've watched baseball on color television you've probably seen granulated brick dust. It's used on many major league infields, a product developed from broken building materials. It's certainly colorful and can liven up a drab area as a ground cover. But, like sand, it tends to sog down in damp weather and requires raking to keep it looking fresh. Make sure to get the granulated texture, not dust. Dust can blow over your fence during the next windstorm.

Shredded Tree Bark: This is the only vegetable-derived material on our list, though others could be added. Any of the mulches discussed in the Flower Section could serve as ground cover on a temporary basis, but tree bark is more resistant to decay. You can buy it in sizes ranging from a half to two inches in diameter (depending on the texture you prefer) and you can expect several years of use (especially from Redwood) before it begins to decompose. Many people choose tree bark *because* of its vegetable origin. They feel it's more appropriate to a garden setting than mineral materials. A word of caution though. Like raw sawdust, untreated tree bark tends to rob soils of nitrogen as it disintegrates, so you'll have to supply extra feedings of high nitrogen fertilizer to compensate your plants for this loss.

River-washed Pebbles: These polished, egg-shaped pebbles are collected from river washes and beaches. They vary in color, depending on the rock from which they originated. Some, from basalt, are jet black; others are white, streaked and veined in red. Browns, buffs, blues, and grays fill in the range between. A mixture of larger pebbles (one to three inches in diameter) makes an excellent, low maintenance ground cover. The stones are heavy enough to be stable and most leaves and dirt can be washed off at the end of a hose. Debris which still lingers can be whisked out with the household vacuum. River-washed pebbles can create an eye-catching feature in any garden; so much so that they should be used with restraint. Cost is another realistic restraining factor.

HOW TO BUY INERT GROUND COVERS

Your Garden Center will probably stock some of the foregoing materials in packaged sizes. Shredded tree bark is usually sold in bags holding four cubic feet, and river-washed pebble in one-cubic-foot sacks. If your needs are small, load up and drive on home. But if you want to cover a considerable area, it's a great saving to buy in "loose" (unpackaged) bulk.

Your salesman may be able to arrange delivery to your home from his own supply source; or he may direct you down the road to a Builders' Materials and Supply yard. In either case, you'll want to know exactly how much ground cover to order, and that means measuring and figuring.

In our sketch we show an irregular-shaped bed planted with low-growing Junipers. We resolve the shape into an approximate rectangle, measuring 30 by 35 feet. Multiplying, we find the area is roughly 1050 square feet.

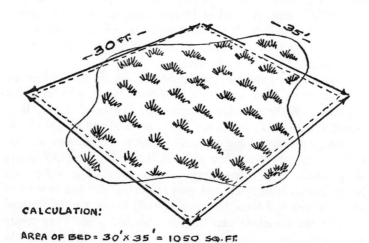

CALCULATION:

AREA OF BED = 30' x 35' = 1050 SQ. FT.

MATERIAL (AT 2 INCH DEPTH) = $\frac{1050}{6}$ = 175 CUBIC FT.

MATERIAL (IN CUBIC YDS.) = $\frac{175}{27}$ = 6½ CUBIC YDS.

You want to apply your inert ground cover 2 inches deep. Two inches is ⅙th of a foot. Therefore, dividing by 6, we arrive at 175 cubic feet—the bulk of material you'll need.

One step more is necessary—a resolution into cubic yards—the form in which most bulk materials are sold. Divide by 27 (27 cubic feet in a cubic yard) and the answer comes out at approximately 6½ cubic yards.

The material will be trucked (at a reasonable extra charge) to your home and, unless you put up a fierce protest, dumped squarely in the middle of your driveway, possibly trapping your car in the garage. (A fierce protest will get it dumped in the street, if that's permitted by your local ordinances.) After that, disposal is up to you and your wheelbarrow.

Chapter 29

YOUR EXISTING GROUND COVERS

Possibly you already own ground covers and are far from convinced that they're the answer to the Lazy Gardener's low maintenance prayer. Your Ivy may be running rampant, climbing trees and walls and encroaching on your lawn. You may have planted Myrtle on a bank to stop erosion and it's failed to do the job. Each year there's less Myrtle and less bank. If that's the best ground covers can do, what's to cheer for?

Let's begin by making sure of our facts. Are you certain that invasive plant *is* Ivy? Virginia Creeper looks somewhat similar and Ivy often gets blamed for its misbehavior. Does your "Ivy" turn red in autumn, then lose its leaves? Sounds suspiciously like Virginia Creeper. Cut off a runner and show it to your Garden Center expert just to make sure. If it *is* Virginia Creeper, you may as well plan on getting rid of it. You'll never be able to control well-established vines in a small area. Spray the leaves with a 2-4-D solution and keep spraying new growth which may appear until you're sure the vine is dead. Clean out the debris, work the soil, and start afresh with a ground cover better suited to the location.

Of course, it *could* be Ivy—a long-neglected mat that's been allowed to run wild. Your job will be to tame it. Wait till spring is well advanced, then cut all stems and woody growth back to the roots. Fertilize the stubble with blood meal and water heavily. In a few weeks, a neat and orderly array of new leaves should appear to delight you.

The same technique of "cutting back" can be applied to most herbaceous ground covers which have become unkempt and shabby. Like all perennials, they regenerate from their root systems and benefit from trimming of their tops. You can't be quite as drastic in pruning overgrown woody shrubs but, by selected cutting, much can be done to restore neatness.

Now let's look at those unsatisfactory Myrtles—also called Periwinkles or Vincas in different localities. Can you honestly say you gave them a fair chance? You can hardly expect new roots— even ground cover roots—to perform successfully on steeply sloping ground without assistance. Every time it rains, or you turn on the sprinklers, water cuts away their foundations, washing them out.

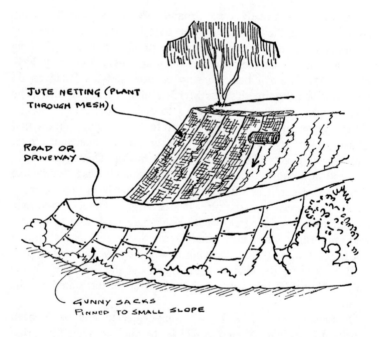

JUTE NETTING (PLANT THROUGH MESH)

ROAD OR DRIVEWAY

GUNNY SACKS PINNED TO SMALL SLOPE

Let's try planting those Myrtles again, using different techniques.

If the bank you're dealing with is large (over two thousand square feet, say) you'll probably need jute netting to stabilize your planting. Jute netting can be bought in rolls which are eased, strip by strip, down a slope. You pin each strip in place with wire staples, then cut the roll and climb the hill for the next downward unraveling. After covering the bank with netting, you plant Myrtle through the mesh.

CUT WIRE CLOTHES HANGER AT
4 POINTS: A, B, C AND D TO MAKE 4 STAPLES.

If you're dealing with a smaller bank, you can use old gunny sacks in place of the netting. Split them open for maximum spread and pin them to the slope with staples cut from wire clothes hangers (the sketch shows you how). When the bank is covered, slit the sacking with a sharp knife and plant the Myrtle through the holes.

Both netting and sacking will prevent soil erosion and provide stable conditions for root development. If you're in a hurry to see your Myrtles grow, you might spray them every six weeks with liquid fertilizer—after the plants are established.

Possibly you consider old gunny sacks unsightly. If so, have patience. Within a couple of seasons they'll disappear from view, covered by Myrtle green. In time the sacks will rot away but, if all has gone well, you'll be totally unaware of their passing.

Ground covers are invaluable for holding slopes, filling hollows, and carpeting ground where nothing else will grow. But these are utilitarian functions. As we have suggested, ground covers also have design values which are too often overlooked. Deftly employed, they can alter the appearance of your garden setting—sometimes quite dramatically.

We'll explore some of these possibilities in the next chapter.

Chapter 30

NEW USES FOR GROUND COVERS

Let's assume you've put your front yard into tiptop shape. Your trees are tiered with leaves. Your shrubs are pruned and perky. Your lawn is a velvet meadow of pest-free, unfungused green. Yet you're vaguely dissatisfied with the looks of the place. It's too plain somehow, lacking in interest. All the garden elements are there, but they seem scattered, unrelated to each other or the house.

What's wrong?

It could be that a central design idea is missing. There's no inducement for the eye to follow a pleasing composition which would unify the dispersed elements.

Let's go outside and look at your front yard with fresh eyes. If your home was built as part of a development during the last decade, chances are good that your front yard was laid out as a rectangle. The house stands back, parallel to the sidewalk. The driveway runs on a beeline for the garage. Your front walk—if it's separated from the driveway—makes another beeline for the front steps. Probably a pavement joins driveway and front walk close to the house, paralleling it. In short, every man-made shape which faces us is a rigid rectangle. Only your trees and shrubs give a feeling of roundness, naturalness, and flow.

Your front yard may very well follow the plan diagrammed below:

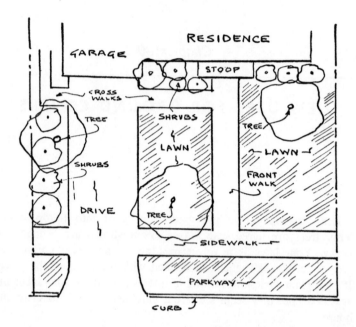

Our focus, as we look at your home from the sidewalk, is your front door. Our eyes are drawn toward it by the long walk, the placement of the trees, and the break in the shrubbery at either side of the stoop. But our way of reaching your front door—up the straight and narrow path—fails to invite us.

Why?

The answer, of course, must be based on pyschological values—made more complicated by the fact that no two people, viewing your home, would react psychologically in exactly the same way. Still, under the given conditions, we might hazard the following guesses as to why your front walk fails to attract us.

1. It's too long and straight (uninteresting).
2. It's too cold (concrete is a "cold" material).
3. It's too impersonal (it looks like a branch of the sidewalk—there's no feeling of entering *your* garden, leading to *your* home).

4. It's unadventurous (the solid lawn on either side gives the feeling of walking through a public park).

Other negative reactions could be added but, hopefully, we've made our point. The question is, what can be done about it? Is there a way to provide a more inviting entrance to your home short of tearing out sidewalk and landscaping and starting afresh?

Possibly—through the creative use of ground covers.

Perhaps we can best illustrate this by redesigning your front yard in several different ways. In each case, we'll alter only the rectangular blocks of your lawn. Trees and shrubs remain untouched.

Study the following three sketches to decide whether their suggestions might increase the welcoming atmosphere of your home for future visitors. Meanwhile we'll tiptoe out, to meet you again on a later page.

1.

2.

3.

Hello, there!

Now that you've studied the sketches, let's return to that list of negative reactions to see if redesigning has improved matters.

The original objections to your front walk—and possible answers—are as follows:

1. It's too long and straight.

It's still just as long but, hopefully, the eye has been distracted by the sweep of ground covers to make the walk *seem* shorter. There's something to hold the attention besides counting steps.

2. It's too cold.

It's the same old concrete, but ground cover textures and flowers should "warm" it up.

3. It's too impersonal.

Unless every house on the block decides to redesign with ground covers, your front yard should stand out as distinctly different.

4. It's unadventurous.

With any luck, your front walk should convey the feeling of cutting through a flower-edged meadow. To get really fanciful, the distant goal—your front stoop—may seem an inviting promontory up which to climb.

If you still have doubts about psychological factors, look again at the prettiest garden you know, or the best landscaped public building. There's something about the composition of plants and structures which you find pleasing. What is it? What is the guiding idea behind the design which pulls all the elements into a harmonious whole? It's not always easy to distinguish, but at least you can be sure of one thing—someone was concerned about what you'd think and feel when you saw the place for the first time.

OTHER GROUND COVER DESIGN SITUATIONS

Of course, your own front yard may not take the form of a rectangle pierced by a concrete walk. You may live on an L-shaped lot on a corner. Or a curve in the street may face you with an oval entrance. Your house may not be built on flat land, but up on a hill or down in a dale. In any event, you may still feel dissatisfied with the approach to your home and wonder what you can do about it.

We don't suggest that ground covers are the magic answer for every design problem. Some are too complicated for simplified solutions. But at least ground covers offer a practical method for diverting the eye from the negative aspects of your garden to the positive.

Begin your analysis by retracing the steps we previously took together. Go out to the sidewalk and look back at your home with fresh eyes. Imagine you're a visitor making his way up your front walk for the first time. What would he think and feel?

Be absolutely honest with yourself. You'll get nowhere by protecting your ego.

List negative reaction on paper. The simple act of writing them down often suggests solutions. As ideas occur to you, sketch out how they might look when executed in your garden. If you're not talented with a pencil, perhaps others in the family are and will share your interest in the project. After all, it's their home too.

When you've reached your solutions, don't feel you have to rush for your shovel. Torn-up lawns—and uprooted shrubs, if you're ambitious—are troublesome to replace. "Live" with your ideas for a while, imagining their effect every time you turn in your front walk. You'll probably make adjustments during this last phase—for convenience, or other practical reasons.

When you're completely sure, *then* move, and move fast. You remember what happened to Lot's wife when she looked back. You don't want that to happen to you. Salt is very damaging in garden soils.

CHOOSING YOUR GROUND COVERS

Obviously you will choose ground covers which bloom at different periods in order to extend floral effects throughout the growing season. But just as important as flowers are leaf color, texture, and size considerations.

For instance, Cotton Lavender—and most shrub ground covers —provides bold accents which can project an area into prominence. Ajuga, Yellow Cinquefoil, and Creeping Thyme are "carpet" growers which don't call attention to themselves but please by their hues and textures—as do many inert ground covers.

Be careful of such vivid performers as Moss Pink and Basket-of-gold in their flowering seasons. Place them where you want the eye to be drawn for a brilliant month in late spring—beside a handsome wall, perhaps, or under a still leafless tree—but don't let them conflict with a fine Dogwood in bloom or the color load of a Forsythia.

In general, try to use the mass-blossoming ground covers with restraint. There's a difference between the floral effect of a perennial or annual garden in full bloom and the blankets of color which can emanate from some ground covers. The eye can assimilate and mix the former, but tends to be blasted by the latter. Gaudy sunsets are grand in nature, but you only see them once in a long while. You see your garden every day and too much strong color can be jarring, like a badly reproduced picture postcard.

Chapter 31

GROUND COVER MISCELLANY

(Planting, Fertilization, Irrigation, Pests and Diseases, Weed Control)

It's an indication of the trouble-free nature of ground covers that we can compress into one chapter a variety of maintenance topics which sometimes required a detailed chapter each in previous sections in this book. To repeat a thought developed earlier, ground covers are rugged plants, delighted to take care of themselves in the easy living of your garden after centuries of roughing it in the wilds. They're not demanding of your time and attention —in fact, perform best when not pampered—a characteristic to stir applause from any Lazy Gardener.

PLANTING HERBACEOUS GROUND COVERS

Herbaceous ground covers are usually sold in quantity lots. Your Garden Center may handle them in wooden flats, each growing fifty to a hundred small plants. Or your salesman may simply go out into the nursery section and dig up a clump. When you get home, you'll carefully separate the clump, disentangling the roots of individual plants, before you put them in the ground.

Ground covers are usually planted from six to eighteen inches "on center" (meaning the space between plants), depending on growth vigor and eventual size. Check with your salesman on the recommended distance for the plants you buy. Set them out in a diamond pattern. This insures light and air while the roots are catching hold, and also tends to prevent erosion channels from opening up.

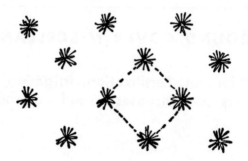

Diamond planting pattern

Though in nature nobody tills the soil for ground covers, it's advisable in your garden to prepare their beds as carefully as you would for perennial flowers (Chapter 24). This isn't an absolute "must," but it helps get ground covers off to a fast start, which hastens the day when you can forget about them (almost).

FERTILIZATION

The trick with herbaceous ground covers is to feed them as *seldom* as possible. Overfertilization stimulates excessive top growth which detracts from neatness. How often is seldom? Once a year is usually enough—just before blossoming to promote a full floral effect. Ground covers which bloom all summer would benefit from a second feeding later in the season.

Shrub ground covers can use more fertilizer, especially new plantings. Your purpose here is different; you're trying to speed growth to cover bare ground. A six-week schedule, from March to September, isn't too much for shrubs. Stop in September, though. Lush growth which develops later is subject to winter freeze.

Use blood meal for both herbaceous and shrub feedings. Sprinkle it over the matted ground covers and wash it through the leaves immediately afterwards. Place a handful over the root area of each woody shrub and water in.

IRRIGATION

When herbaceous plants are first put into the ground, make sure the soil is kept damp; a daily wetting with a fine spray may be necessary in times of drought. Once they are established, water is dispensable, since crowding tops shade the ground against evaporation. Few ground covers need more water than falls as rain, even in an off year. Don't spoil them by offering extra drinks.

This principle holds true even for the Southwest where rainfall from May to September is so rare as to call out crowds. Native ground covers—Carmel Creeper and Coyote Bush, to name two —can exist through an entire summer without taxing your sprinkler system (though they look better for a monthly soaking). This waterless rule doesn't apply, of course, to imported ground covers (which most are, in arid regions), but a weekly irrigation is usually enough for their needs.

PESTS AND DISEASES

In order to survive in the wilderness, herbaceous ground covers seem to have developed juices distasteful to pests. At least you'll rarely find yourself galloping with a spray gun to quell an uprising of chewing or sucking insects. Ground cover foliage, however, sometimes provides a hiding place for slugs and snails. They snooze in this cool shelter during the day, then sally forth at night to munch your lawn or prized shrubs. Poison bait gets rid of them, though, in fairly short order.

Fungus can occasionally be an irritant, especially in warm winter climates where the long season causes top growth to pile up. If you see telltale indications of browning, clean out plant tops through the area and apply a fungicide.

In general, most herbaceous creeping ground covers benefit from a prophylactic top clipping in early spring. In areas of winter ice (jokingly called the Temperate Zone) there isn't much alternative to shearing off the blackened tops which melting snow reveals. But even in warm winter regions, some trimming improves neatness, health, and the later display of flowers.

WEED CONTROL

Since a major asset of mature ground covers is to smother weeds and save you work, you probably won't begrudge the time necessary to keep their beds cleaned out while they're struggling to establish themselves. You'll know that, soon enough, no weed seed will be able to germinate in the darkness beneath their leaves.

With inert ground covers it's a different story. Once weeds penetrate the loose materials, they can become a perpetual nuisance. You can keep them in check with herbicides, but constant spraying is a nuisance too.

Perhaps the best way to handle the situation is to install a ground sheet *before* you lay the materials. A heavy duty polyethylene is best for this purpose. It comes in rolls and is easy and light to manipulate.

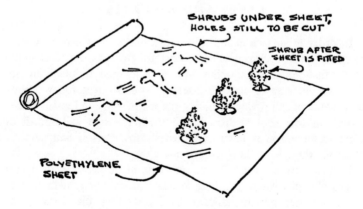

Controlling weeds with polyethylene sheets

Grade out the area to be covered, then spread the polyethylene over it, sheet overlapping sheet. If shrubs have already been planted, cut out holes and slip the sheets over their heads. The holes should be large enough to permit water and fertilizers to reach plant roots.

When the entire area is neatly plastered with sheets, dump the inert ground cover on top of it and smooth out. The polyethylene material will hold up for a good many years and, while it does, no weed is likely to penetrate. Just one caution: Don't try to lay ground sheets on a windy day—the flapping is worse than being caught in a hen run when a hawk appears.

INDEX